THE LADY FARMER
GUIDE TO SLOW LIVING

CULTIVATING SUSTAINABLE SIMPLICITY
CLOSE TO HOME

By Mary E. Kingsley

Illustrated by Eileen M. Schaeffer

LADY FARMER, LLC
L | 🌱 | F

Copyright © 2020 by Lady Farmer, LLC

All rights reserved. This book or any portion thereof may not be reproduced or used in any manner whatsoever without the express written permission of the publisher except for the use of brief quotations in a book review.

Lady Farmer is a registered trademark of Lady Farmer, LLC

Printed in the United States of America

Illustrations by Eileen M. Schaeffer
Book Design by Christopher Fisher
Cover Design by ebooklaunch.com
Back Cover Photo by Meaghan White, meaghanclarephotography.com

ISBN 978-0-578-41595-6

Lady Farmer, LLC
PO Box 651
Poolesville, MD 20837
(651) 347-4369

https://www.lady-farmer.com/
https://twitter.com/weareladyfarmer
https://www.instagram.com/weareladyfarmer/
https://www.facebook.com/weareladyfarmer/
https://www.pinterest.com/ladyfarmerusa/

Phrases such as *slow food, slow living, slow fashion, slow spaces*, and so on are used by the author as general terms for the movement toward ethical, responsible, sustainable processes intended to improve both human and planetary well-being. Lady Farmer, LLC, is not affiliated with any specific entity which uses these terms, although some of these entities may be referenced in the text or listed as resources.

For Lady Farmers everywhere, all of you who are sowing the seeds of slow living for yourselves and those around you. Whether you are cultivating country acreage or a life in the city, tending a garden, a family or a career, we hold you in highest regard and celebrate you and your desire to create space in your life for more sustainable living. May you all find peace, joy, and slowness amidst the sacred work of healing the planet.

Contents

Introduction — 1
Sowing Seeds of Slow Living — 3
Reflections — 9

Section One: Slow Food — 13
Why Slow Food? — 15
Slow Food Is Real Food — 19
Slow Food is Local Food — 27
Slow Food is Live Food — 45
Section One Reflections — 57

Section Two: Slow Fashion — 59
From Seed to Sewn to Sold — 61
Seed: Farm to Closet — 65
Sewn: Fabric Sourcing & Manufacturing — 69
Sold: A Good Price — 77
Section Two Reflections — 81

Section Three: Slow Spaces 83
Shelter 85
Surroundings 89
Stuff 91
Section Three Reflections 105

Conclusion 107
The Earth As Our Home 109

List of Resources 111

21 Day Slow-Living Shift 117

About the Author 141

Works Cited 143

Introduction

Sowing Seeds of Slow Living

So what is slow living? Why are people talking about it so much these days, and why is it important?

Our own understanding of slow living has to do, quite simply, with making conscious choices about how we live our lives. It's about paying attention to how we spend our time, money and resources, and taking a step back from the industrialized systems that have come to provide our daily needs. It's also about observing our own consumer habits, where and how they intersect with quality of life and perpetuate an unsustainable paradigm.

What we offer in this book are our own observations for reflection and discussion, practical suggestions, and perhaps some gentle guidance stemming from our own thoughts and experience as residents of this planet who are inclined to ponder such things.

We are not doctors, so please understand that nothing we put forth should be considered above the advice of your preferred medical professional. Nor are we degreed historians, economists or social analysts, however we do make every effort to gather our data from reliable sources, to be informed, observant and discerning.

One doesn't have to be a professional anything to witness how quickly our society has shifted in the last two generations. Some of us can look back in our own lives or those of our parents or grandparents to recall a time when people weren't dependent on factory farms thousands of miles away for their food, nor on chain stores for cheap clothing made overseas by impoverished workers. Many grew their own food and made their clothing, or at least obtained them from a known source; and until well into the 20th century many Americans did all of this without electrical power in their homes.

It has been less than a century since Americans were largely self-sufficient producers of many of their daily needs and moderate consumers of the rest. In the "waste not, want not" days of our grandparents or great-grandparents, responsible use of resources was not only enforced through rationing (especially during WWII) but also seen as a citizen's patriotic duty.

Fast forward to now, when practically every single thing we use is bought from a store (or Amazon) and is excessively packaged, taped, safety sealed, shrink-wrapped, encased in plastic, tamper-proofed ... and on and on. Think about this as you move through your everyday tasks, actually looking at the products, containers, tools, and implements we use from morning till night, and contemplate where it came from, how it got into your hands, what's in it and how much waste was created from it before you even owned it. *(I often find myself reflecting on these questions while trying to OPEN something—and not very patiently, I might add.)* Most of these things are used up or broken in a relatively short period of time, after which their packaging, containers and carcasses are mindlessly tossed into the land of "trash," that place our society assumes is the endpoint of our concern.

We have evolved from a more "circular" mindset in our consumer behavior (one that is conscious of limited resources and encourages conservation and restoration) to a full-on "linear" economy, in which we are addicted to our need for cheap, mass-produced goods that have only one direction to go—from production to use to disposal in a landfill.

Our food supply, too, has long left the realm of self-production and now has much more connection to a factory or a lab than the land. It has been sprayed, machinated, wrapped, frozen, fortified, processed, sealed, flown around the globe, clam-shelled and shelved until we, full collaborators in this paradigm, happily pull these things from the supermarket aisles in the name of sustenance. As for our clothing, almost everything available for purchase today has been produced at a terrible cost to not only the environment and our health, as we shall see, but also to the overworked and underpaid hands that put them together, all so that we can indulge our manic, throwaway habits while barely making a dent in our pocketbooks.

In recent decades, time and money are two things that consumers want to save over anything else, giving rise to the attraction of convenience, the almighty "bargain," fast food and fast fashion. How and when these perceived shortages became such a driving force in our society is probably beyond the scope of this discussion, but recognizing these cultural shifts is essential to understanding their impact.

The truth is that we have the same amount of time as did our ancestors and our grandparents. The difference is in how we choose to spend it. As we have come to understand it, the slow living choice to feed and clothe ourselves closer to the source doesn't necessarily take *less* time or work or money. In some instances it might take more. Those that have made the conscious decision to eat more locally know this. It takes effort and organization to seek out local sources and very often, requires us to pay more. Supermarkets might offer organic produce but it often isn't local or fresh and very few offer meat options that are not from CAFO (concentrated animal feeding operation) sources. Growing your own is a wonderful option but is a commitment as well. During growing season when we're planting and weeding the garden plot and trying to keep it all going through drought, and at the end of the summer when our cup runneth over with wonderful things from the garden that need to be harvested, prepared and preserved—life is not "slow," as in "leisurely." There is a huge amount of effort and energy involved. Yet, this is the choice we make over driving to the megamarket and buying packaged and processed food that could be on the table and ready to eat in no time.

We call that slow living.

Likewise, the slow living choice for clothing that has not been produced at the expense of the land, our water, another human's well-being and our own health certainly will cost more in terms of dollars and cents. The reality is that many people aren't able to buy clothes that are made from responsibly sourced materials and well-paid workers. The prevailing fast fashion system has squeezed the life out of this model and the availability of ethically produced apparel is extremely limited, putting the majority of consumers in a position where they feel they have no choice.

Yet this is the crucial point. Anyone and everyone *can* become aware that there might be another choice, that there *should* be a choice other than participating in the prevailing paradigm of addiction, oppression, pollution and poisons.

Thomas Berry, cultural historian and twentieth century visionary, sums up what he believes to be the "Great Work" of humankind as we move into the new century. It is "*to carry out the transition from a period of human devastation of the Earth to a period when humans would be present to the planet in a mutually beneficial manner.*"[1]

Uncovering these shadows in our society and educating consumers on the realities of the systems we have been unconsciously supporting is the path to change and, in our way of thinking, the heart of slow living.

We can do this, each and every one of us, in small ways, in seemingly minuscule decisions, in the example we set for those around us. We don't have to be loud or preachy, or "holier than thou." No single behavior is going to be right for everyone. We all got here together even if we came from a thousand different directions. The way out is with individual changes, but the ultimate paradigm-shifting changes will be collective.

Our goal in exploring the idea of slow living is to identify where we have become separated from "the hand that feeds us," so to speak, and to find our way back to a right relationship with the true source of our nurturance. We want to see ourselves apart from mass production and consumption, hear our own voice inside the noisy torrent of information, and seek out the things we truly value. In that space, perhaps, is where we reclaim our allotted time on the planet and create our truly authentic lives.

To help you in your own exploration of slow living, we've provided some questions and suggestions for reflection at the end of each section. We hope you'll use these only in ways that seem helpful to you, remembering that you alone are the one true expert on your own life. So come join us in whatever way feels right. It's good to be waking up.

Reflections

1. Think about your relationship to food, clothing and shelter (your home and spaces). Spend a few minutes journaling about each one individually. Here are some questions to help you in this exercise, but let this take you where it wants to go.

> **Food:** Considering you and food, is it a friendly relationship? Have you ever struggled with it, in terms of health or weight issues, eating disorders, eating too much or too little? Do you like to prepare food for yourself and those around you, or is it something you prefer to spend little time thinking about? How do you navigate all of the confusing information about food that's out there? Do you adhere to the restrictions of any particular diets or philosophies? What would you like to change about your relationship to food?

> **Clothing:** How does one describe a relationship to their clothing? There's a lot there when you think about it. Go back to your childhood; how did you feel about clothes then? Did you feel you always had the right clothes in school, or were you insecure about how to dress and fit in? Were there frustrations with fashion and body issues? What habits did you develop around acquiring your clothes? Was it generally a positive or negative experience? Did you go shopping? Did you or someone else make them? What has changed about

how you acquire your clothes and how you feel about them? Do you have enough? Too many? Is shopping something you do for entertainment or out of necessity? What would you like to change about your relationship to clothing?

Spaces: What can you say about where you live? Do you feel at home there? Are you comfortable with it? In it? What's the story of where you now reside? How long have you been there and how long do you foresee staying there? What are your favorite spaces within it? Are there spaces that cause you irritation or anxiety? Do you have other spaces outside of your home that feel good? Where do you spend most of your time away from home? If you go to a job, what is your feeling about that space? Do you have a desk or a cubicle? Describe what that's like for you. What would you like to change about your relationship to the spaces in your life?

Reflect on the fact that your body is a space that you inhabit that needs food, clothing and shelter. How might unresolved issues with your primary needs affect you in other areas of your life?

2. As you think about slow living in your own life, what ideas, images and associations immediately come to mind? Capture these initial impressions in your head, in writing or even by drawing them out so that you can more closely observe the ideas that might be guiding you in this quest. Isolate them and ask yourself where they come from. What comes from deep within you? What is a true longing vs. an ego need? How are these impressions informed by social media or current trends?

Cultivate the images and scenarios that bring you the most joy and delight, spend time with them, keep them handy and bring them to mind whenever possible.

3. Keep in mind that no matter where we are, we're always headed somewhere, and everything that happens on the way is called LIFE. I heard a story once, and though I can't say where it came from, it made an impression on me. So I will share a version of it here.

> *A man was walking along the side of the road when a car pulled up beside him. A younger man leaned out from the driver's seat and asked, "Where you headed?"*
> *"Into town."*
> *"So am I! Would you like a ride?"*
> *"What for?"*
> *"To get there faster!"*
> *The older man stopped and turned to the driver. He seemed honestly bewildered.*
> *"Why would I want to do that?" he asked.*
> *"To save time, of course," said the younger, trying not to laugh. But now it was the old man's turn to laugh.*
> *"Son," he said, shaking his head. "Don't you know ... you can't save time. You can only decide how you're going to spend it."*

This story reminds me that the "getting there" can be as precious as the "there," that idea we hold in our hearts and minds as the accomplishment of our efforts. Like our consumer mentality, our dreams and goals sometimes take on a linear quality. We want to get somewhere or have something that takes our awareness out of our present experience.

4. Reflect on some of your most treasured memories and experiences and where each one fits into that journey/destination continuum. Are they one or the other, or do they have aspects of both? What happens when we apply a more circular mindset in this area of our lives as well?

Section One: Slow Food

Why Slow Food?

"If it's a plant, eat it. If it was made in a plant, don't."
—Michael Pollan[2]

Human life has always revolved around food as one of our most basic needs. Yet our present day relationship to daily sustenance bears little resemblance to that of our early ancestors. For the nomadic, hunter-gatherer societies predating agriculture, the procurement of nourishment was the primary activity. Then, with the agricultural revolution, human communities began to stay in one place where they could grow a reliable food supply and domesticate animals for meat and for labor. The daily life of humans changed radically as civilization evolved with the rise of villages, cities and trade-based economies.

It's important to understand how recently this shift has occurred. There are many theories as to how long humans have been on the planet, some estimates of our ancestors going back four to six million years[3] and those closest to modern humans dating from around 200,000 years ago or more.[4] With agriculture beginning perhaps 10,000-12,000 years ago[5] (theories vary), it's clear that humans have been growing their food for only a fraction of the time they've been on the planet.

Early humans had a different connection to the earth as the source of their sustenance. As a species, we have a much longer history of obtaining food from the existing ecosystems, as in hunting wild animals in their habitat and foraging plants out of the natural environment. When we started growing crops, the connection shifted from a partnership with the system (leave it intact and figure out survival within it) to a conquest-and-dominate-the-land model. In other words, humans began trying to adapt nature to their own needs rather than the other way around.

Anthropologists aren't sure why humans started farming, whether it was climate change or food shortages, but it sparked a tremendous growth in the population and signaled the beginning of the global topsoil depletion that we are now facing. Instead of following herds of animals, humans migrated in search of land. We see it in the history of our country and the agrarian vision of our founding fathers, the yearning for space and expansion, the desire for independence, roots and self-sufficiency. The Homestead Act of 1862 opened up the west for settlement by offering 160 acres to any American, including free slaves, willing to improve the land, build a house and grow crops. By the 1930's, more than 270 million acres had been handed to over 1.6 million homestead applicants.[6] This was over ten percent of all US lands.

In the last century, however, agriculture has veered dramatically from the model of individuals producing food on a small scale for their families and communities and has become the domain of giant industries who grow for the masses. Food (and everything else) is something not garnered by our own spear, hands, or hoe—but obtained with currency. As we see today, the goods we buy in the grocery store have been grown, packaged and shipped from every corner of the world and brought to us, who buy and consume readily without thought of the source, methods or process. From an evolutionary standpoint, to come to this point from the ways of our relatively recent nomadic ancestors has been a very sudden shift.

This system has caused great harm not only to the collective health of our human bodies but also to our earth body as well. The once rich topsoil that covered the earth and offered its inhabitants a wealth of abundant nutrients has been gradually used up. Now we need chemicals to make things grow in this depleted soil, substances that are derived primarily from fossil fuels. The food that is grown by such methods (the majority of food grown worldwide) cannot offer humans many of the needed nutrients that we require for optimum health. Industrial food production has altered the nutritional components of the SAD (standard American diet) to such a degree that as a population, we are in many ways malnourished. That's why so many are diseased, starving, obese, depressed and unhappy.

Thus we find ourselves in this moment of our human history, realizing we have become so separated from the source of a most fundamental need that we are sick and sorrowful at a level even beyond our own understanding. Yet we are not hopeless. There is so much we can do for ourselves, our families and our communities to reclaim who we are in relation to our earth and our bodies in this life journey. We have such a yearning to fill an emptiness where our connection to the source used to be that we are literally building communities around it. Most of us don't envision a complete return to our nomadic roots or an off-the-grid homesteading lifestyle, although there are those that do and we encourage them. But as we all know, the world is different now and whichever way we choose in all of this, we have to move forward with consciousness and knowledge.

Mary E. Kingsley

That's what slow food is about, to bring ourselves back into health and harmony with this most fundamental aspect of our being. We'll learn from each other and apply what we can to our own situations. The steps may be small but each one is rich in reward and brings us closer to healing.

Slow Food Is Real Food

For my breakfast this morning, I had plain, whole milk yogurt sprinkled with pomegranate seeds, walnuts, cinnamon and honey. It took a while to separate the luscious seeds from their tight little clumps inside the fruit, and as I was doing so I thought about how the cows had grazed the hillsides to produce the grass-fed milk and how millions of tiny bacteria had spent their lives culturing it into yogurt. Then there was a tree that grew for years and years before growing these delicious walnuts, and there were the bees that traveled so many miles and visited so many thousands of flowers to create this perfect little bit of sweetness for me, this morning, and I thought about food and the time it takes and how we often try so hard to get around that.

I grew up in a time when Carnation Instant Breakfast was the latest and greatest thing, along with TANG and Pop Tarts, products inspired by the Space Age. We were awestruck by images of the Gemini astronauts floating around in zero gravity sucking their nutrients in the form of powders and pastes delivered through tubes going straight to their mouths. They had so much to do up there in those capsules, exploring the universe and so on, and there was no such thing as "sitting" down for a meal in a weightless environment. It made perfect sense that this was how they would eat. Of course *we* wanted to be like the astronauts because we were busy too, and taking the time to actually sit down for breakfast before dashing out the door to school seemed so "way back when."

The food industry complied with our fascination for instant, minimal preparation sustenance by creating countless "open and eat" products convenient for a busy lifestyle. Most people (many moms included) thought this was okay as long as we were getting the nutrients we needed, which we thought we were. After all, it said so on the box.

Years later I brought this assumption into my own family life as standard operating procedure, though thinking I was being discerning, I always read labels and looked for things that were high protein, low fat, and vitamin fortified. I trusted in modern science that nutrients created in a lab would do the job, and that as long as we followed the USDA Food Pyramid guidelines we were eating well. But creating a meal with the four food groups and having the family gather around the table to eat it every night was a pipe dream. Occasionally? *Sure.* Normal? *Nope.* After all, there was school, homework, and the myriad after-school demands on our time ... dance, drama, tennis, music, scouts, softball, concerts, recitals ... you name it.

Convenience was the name of the game when it came to meals. It was the same for most families of the time I think, and perhaps still is, but nevertheless I don't like admitting it. I think about these things and write about them as a way of bringing about change, for myself as well as for others who might be interested. The slow food movement is evidence of a growing awareness of how our food systems have failed us. Remembering the instant breakfast days, I consciously allow myself the moments needed to prepare my slow breakfast, and then savor the milk, fruit and honey flavors that can only be created and enjoyed with time.

Our slow food journey includes our garden here at Three Graces Farm, now in its eighth year. As with everything else, it's a work in progress, guided mostly by the same impulse that brought us here to the farm eight years ago—to live, eat and play close to the earth. There hasn't been much of a plan, but more an evolution of one idea after another.

We've grown the space over the seasons by covering sections of the pasture behind the house with a deep mulch comprised of wood chips, delivered free of charge from a local tree service. With enough depth, the weeds and watering are kept to a minimum and the soil beneath is slowly enriched as the wood chips break down and release nutrients over the course of years.

I consider the space as an experiment in permaculture, a system that (ideally) minimizes human intervention and maximizes the hands-free role of Mother Nature going about her business. The intended result is a low-maintenance and largely perennial (comes back year after year) source of food, flowers, herbs and medicinals that increases in yield over time. The applied principles of permaculture[7] serve to restore and regenerate land that has been abused by conventional agriculture over time, but particularly during the last century with the devastating effects of industrial farming.

There is no way of getting around the fact that it takes a while to educate yourself about growing food. Deciding what to plant, where and when is a process that takes place over a succession of seasons. Fruit trees and berry bushes take a few years to get going, and in between are the crazy weather events that can throw you off for an entire cycle. Last spring we had a hard late frost that took out *all* the pears from an already established tree on our property (one that typically yields more than we can even begin to use) and knocked out all of the berries and red currants that I'd expected to see this summer. Once I finally realized that no, they weren't just late, that this year they weren't happening at all, I was able to take the long view. *There's always next year.*

So there is lots of trial and error, sometimes feeling more like error than anything else. For instance, when you realize that in some spots the mulch is so deep that it's really a lot of work getting down to the soil so you can plant things, next time you can apply less! Sometimes the squash bugs will ruin your collards and the raccoons will get the corn. The beans just won't come up, the vine flowers but never fruits, and the apricot seedling that was coming along last spring just up and croaks come summer. You try to find out why and how to fix these things, but mostly you just chalk it up to experience. Yes, we enjoy growing our own food, but I'm learning to enjoy what's working and fill in the gaps at the farmer's market and the groceries that sell the most local produce.

Fortunately, given a few basic guidelines, success in the garden is within most anyone's grasp. That's the good news. There are times when we're able to get our entire meal from our yard (omelets and salad, anyone?) and that's very satisfying. The challenge is when you find yourself with heaps of tomatoes, peppers, squash, beans or whatever it is that decided it would take off that year, enough to feed the throngs. If your goal is to grow food for yourself and your family that's going to last any time beyond the growing season, this is your moment of truth. You've got to do something with it. You can, of course, share the wealth and give it away for others to eat fresh. Beyond that, your choices are to either let it go to waste or preserve it to eat later by canning, dehydrating, freezing or fermenting. And that's why we're here, with inspiration and resources to guide you. All you need is the desire to learn and the willingness to spend a little more time nourishing your body and soul.

Real food is slow food, a gentle journey on our road back to who we are.

A Real Food Staple: Mayonnaise

Mayonnaise is one of America's favorite condiments. It's at the heart of so many of our favorite things. I'm thinking about potato and egg salad, tuna salad and creamy dressings. And what's that leftover turkey sandwich without (a lot of) it?

There was a time, though, when it was a guilty pleasure, especially back in the days when we were all terrified to eat any fats. Then we found out about Sally Fallon and Nourishing Traditions[8] and realized that fats weren't only okay, but we really need them! So we can have all the mayo we want. Right?

But no, because every single one of the brands available in the supermarket is made from tons of creepy ingredients like those industrial vegetable oils and so many other things you can't even pronounce. Store-bought mayonnaise is not a real food. It's like eating chemical goo.

So then we'll just make it ourselves. Right? Well, that sounds good, but every recipe I ever tried requires three hands. You hold the mixer in one, the bowl in the other and then you drop the oil in very slowly, one drop at a time. And if you put the oil in too fast (because it's hard to manage all of this at once) your homemade mayo ends up being a liquid mess and you might even have to start over.

Eating mayonnaise as part of a real food diet was a problem. That is, until I found the following recipe which has changed everything! It's quick, delicious and never fails— like magic.

In fact, the recipe is called "Magic Mayonnaise" and it's in a wonderful book called The Hands-On Home[9] by Erica Strauss.

(NOTE: For this recipe, you need an immersion blender. If you don't already have one of these, I promise you it is worth the small investment. I use mine every single day and consider it my number one kitchen tool.)

Recipe: Real Mayonnaise

In a wide-mouth pint mason jar, combine:

- 1 large egg
- 1 tablespoon fresh lemon juice
- 1 tablespoon white wine vinegar
- 1 teaspoon Dijon mustard
- 1/2 teaspoon salt
- 1 cup neutral-flavored oil (I use a light olive or avocado for mild flavor and to get healthy fats.)

Let the egg settle to the bottom of the jar, then insert the immersion blender all the way down and turn it on at medium speed. Keep it at the bottom so that it will pull the oil down and form an emulsion. When you see that it has become mostly mayonnaise, slowly pull the immersion blender up and out of the jar, pulsing as you go. Put a lid on the jar and it will keep for up to a week.

And that's it.

Quick, easy mayonnaise you can make yourself in five minutes or less, with all healthy, delicious, real food ingredients. So now go have that turkey sandwich with plenty of mayo. Life is good!

Slow Food is Local Food

Has your chicken been to China?

Given the norms of our current industrialized food system, we often don't know how far our food has traveled or how it's been processed, modified or enhanced to survive its journey to our plates.

An extreme example of this is that the USDA allows US-sourced chicken (and seafood) to be shipped to China for processing, and then sent back again for the enjoyment of American consumers. Yes, your lovely Coq Au Vin might well have been around the world and back before passing your lips, but it's been so prepared and preserved you'd never know. But now you *do* know, and that's important.

Almost as bad is the fact that California produces the vast majority of all the fruits, vegetables and nuts consumed in America. If you live on the east coast, that means that those big fat strawberries that look so scrumptious have had a cross country trip (in their plastic, non-biodegradable container) between you and the soil. And that's not the only problem. Apparently, since California is bearing the brunt of such enormous production, the soil is so abused with chemical fertilizers that high levels of nitrogen have tainted the drinking water, putting the local farm worker communities at risk for birth defects, cancer and other health problems.[10] What does that have to say about the food itself? It's enough to make you think twice about that salad bar.

It's a fair bet that most of us don't care for our food to be jetting around the world or taking long road trips on the way to our table. Yet given what's made available in the supermarkets, in many cases it's our only alternative. Unless we are mindful and supportive of our more local food sources, we are reliant on the industrial practices that have come into place over the last half century.

As a rule, the closer food is to its source, the higher the quality and nutritional value. The growing demand for real food has vastly improved our farm-to-table options. With neighborhood farmers' markets, memberships in community supported agriculture (CSA), and supermarkets that feature produce grown within a certain radius, the choice becomes our own. Asking how far the food has traveled before you buy is a powerful step, not only in your own quest for real food, but also in the transformation of a broken system. So even if it's not as close as your own backyard or a neighbor's field, it's more than likely you *don't* have to eat a chicken that's been to China and back.

Meat, Poultry and Dairy

There's plenty of conversation and controversy around meat these days. Should we eat it or not? Does it cause cancer, or is it the best food we have in terms of nutrient density? Is meat production in the US harmful to the environment? Or do the newly emerging regenerative practices in small-scale meat production create opportunities for global topsoil restoration and climate change reversal?

Regardless of personal dietary decisions, everyone needs to know that not all meat choices are alike. The difference between industrialized, factory meat production and pasture raised, 100% grazed animals is like night and day. Only when you have a complete understanding of the nutritional, environmental and humanitarian issues involved in both can you make a fully informed choice for yourself.

First, let's take a look at "modern" or conventionally produced beef. This is what's available through all of the usual outlets, the supermarkets, buying clubs, etc. Unless it clearly states on the label "Organic" or "100% Grass-Fed," then you must assume that it is produced using standard industrial practices. This means that the cows were raised in concentrated animal feeding operations (CAFOs), which is not only an inhumane environment for the animals, but it causes stress hormones to be released into their systems which in turn is present in the meat. They are also fed with grain (GMO corn in most cases), and since cows aren't naturally evolved to eat grain, it makes them sick. That's why they are treated with antibiotics and de-wormers to head off the inevitable infections. The overuse of these substances creates resistant bacteria and parasites in the cows, or "superbugs" that could be passed on to the consumer. Also passed along are the numerous growth hormones that are pumped into the animal in order to fatten them up for the market. Given the rise of childhood obesity and early onset puberty in young girls, a serious question to consider is what those hormones are doing to the humans that eat these products.[11]

Pastured beef, on the other hand, is produced from grazing animals in their natural environment— living, eating and behaving as cows are meant to do. They eat the grasses, herbs and other plants naturally occurring in their habitat which their bodies are designed to ingest and digest efficiently. The result is healthy, contented cows who have little or no need for added hormones, antibiotics, or artificial feed additives because this natural diet is appropriate for their biology. The health and well-being of the animal is passed along to the meat and its consumer. The nutritional benefits of grass-fed beef over modern meat from CAFOs include: increased CLA (conjugated linoleic acids), an animal-sourced nutrient that has been shown to fight cancer; increased Omega-3 oils; reduced heart disease; and blood sugar regulation. Also it's hormone-free, as well as antibiotic- and toxin-free. The nutrition density and complexity of quality pastured beef per ounce cannot be replicated by plants.[12]

What about the environmental concerns? Meat production in the US has been blamed for greenhouse gas emissions, therefore contributing to global warming. But there are other considerations, according to the Environmental Working Group.[13]

> *Well-managed grazing and grass-fed operations are better for the environment. They use fewer energy-intensive inputs and, by regularly moving animals to fresh pasture and keeping them away from streambeds, they spread the manure more evenly and improve the quality and quantity of forage growth. This helps to conserve soil, reduce erosion and water pollution, increase carbon sequestration and preserve biodiversity and wildlife* (Johnson 2002, FAO 2009, Pelletier 2010).

Arguments for plant vs. omnivorous diets based on the resistance to killing animals for food often don't take into account the destructive nature of monoculture (single crop cultivation in a designated area) as a practice, not only to the plant and animal habitat it subjugates but also to the microbial diversity of the planet's already severely depleted topsoil. The widespread assumption that plant-based diets are the better choice for human and planetary health are not addressing the fact that in the current paradigm of global food distribution (with very limited exceptions) plant-based diets are dependent on industrial scale monoculture crop production. The land area used in monoculture cultivation is degraded over time. In the case of grazing animals, however, the habitat and soil biodiversity are protected. The grasslands remain in their natural state and are actually improved in vitality and fertility by the natural biological exchanges between the creatures and the land. Where monoculture cultivation contributes to soil degradation, properly managed pastured grazing facilitates rehabilitation. (The Savory Institute is an excellent source of information on holistic land management. See our "Resources" list.)

The issues with poultry and dairy are similar—overcrowded conditions which cause health problems, necessitating the use of antibiotics and other medications. Organic, pastured chicken is worth the extra cost, especially if you use the bones to make a nourishing broth.[14]

Practices in dairy production, even organic, are highly controversial. Raw milk is far superior[15] in nutrients because pasteurization kills off the living enzymes[16] of this real food, but it's still illegal in many places and very hard to find in others. The important thing if you choose to seek out raw milk is *know your source* and be very confident in their methods. If not processed correctly, it can be dangerous. Fresh, clean raw milk that's been handled carefully, however, is a superfood powerhouse. It's an unfortunate fact that when it comes to raw milk you have to know the realities (both legal and health) and assume your own risk.

As for organic milk, beware the sweet country scenes on the carton that make you think "pure and natural." The organic dairy industry might not be as transparent[17] as we'd like to believe. In some cases, the organic aspect of the product refers to the organic grain fed to the cows. Since cows are not even evolved to eat grain, organic or not (see above), the only benefit to this option is to make the uninformed consumer feel better about the purchase. Your best bet is to reach for the 100% grass-fed varieties over the organic.

Eggs

If you live in a place that allows a chicken or two, then you know that fresh eggs are one of the easiest foods to source for yourself or at a farmers market. The backyard chicken trend is growing for sure, but most people are still getting eggs at the supermarket. As consumers become more aware of common practices in food production (inhumane conditions for animals, hormone/antibiotic use, etc.) the marketing industry tries to create the appeal of a healthy, fresh and natural product. Labels are vague and often misleading, presenting a dizzying array of choices.

Many of the labels are targeted to allay concerns for the treatment of the chickens. Cartons with lovely bucolic country scenes that say "cage free," "free range" and "free roaming" might conjure images of chickens running around gleefully in the grass and sunshine, but it just ain't so. With few exceptions it means they live inside a large building and are free to move around but still with little or no access to the outside. In many cases the outside "access" is a small door somewhere that the chickens never use because they're not raised under natural conditions and probably don't even know what it is, or what the outside is. Though this is better than the conventional factory raised chickens that are confined to a tiny space and can't move at all, it's a far cry from your grandmother's barnyard bird. No sunny skies or cool wind in their feathers for these chickies.

Then there are designations that have to do with the nutritional quality of the eggs. "Natural" is simply a word used to make you feel better about what you are buying. There are no requirements on use of the word, which therefore makes it meaningless in terms of indicating nutrition or quality. You could call almost anything natural, including dirt, sand and poop. You'll see the "Omega-3" label, which means that the chicken feed has been supplemented with flaxseed or fish oil. There is no regulation on this and therefore no accountability to standards, so there's no way of knowing how much the eggs actually contain. It's the same with the label "No Antibiotics or Hormones Used." (More on this here.[18])

The "Certified Organic" label actually does have some meaning, in that the term is regulated to meet certain criteria. Organic eggs are from uncaged chickens that have some access to the outdoors, and are fed an organic vegetarian diet free of animal by-products, pesticides and genetically modified food as regulated by the USDA. However, beak cutting and forced molting is allowed, both issues in the humane treatment category.

This brings us to another point: vegetarian-fed chickens. Chickens are omnivores, which means they eat lots of vegetables *and* proteins (think worms, bugs, slugs, gnats-yum!). Their production of eggs—one of nature's most whole and perfect foods—depends on their consumption of a *complete* diet. That the food industry would try to sell the public on the idea that taking animal proteins away will make the eggs healthier is just plain silly. Proponents of this concept will argue that the non-vegetarian commercial chicken will contain all sorts of nasty animal by-products. This is actually a good point, although it belies the truth of the bigger picture: that "vegetarian" chickens are the invention of a flawed food system, intended to take advantage of the misinformed consumer.[19]

So what's a shopper to do? If I'm standing in front of that vast egg display in the supermarket, I'm looking for the label that says Animal Welfare Approved[20] or Certified Humane.[21] These certifications require the chickens to live and grow outside year round and eat grass, bugs, etc. This is where the eggs get their beta carotene and omega-3's naturally, not from feed supplements. These arguably represent the highest of industry standards.[22]

So, I hope this helps you narrow down all those egg buying options to the few *real* choices. And it goes without saying that the most guaranteed way to get eggs of superior taste and nutritional quality is to go to a source you can verify, a producer that follows the practices most important to you. Most folks these days have access to a farmer's market, a co-op or a CSA, where you can know your grower. If you want the best product, this is your surest bet—unless, of course, you want to get some chickens of your own!

Wild Food

Everybody agrees it's a good idea to eat lots of fruits and vegetables. Eat as many as possible and you'll be getting great nutrition. Right? The answer to that is … well maybe, but certainly not always. Actually, not all fruits and vegetables are created equal. Some have had most of the nutrients cultivated right out of them and others are so full of sugar you'd might as well eat a candy bar.

In her wonderful book called *Eating on the Wild Side*,[23] author Jo Robinson explains how the super-nutritious plants gathered and consumed by our ancestors began to change with the introduction of agriculture. The human preference for sweet and starchy inspired even the earliest farmers to cultivate certain crops over others for taste, leaving astringent, sour and bitter flavored plants in the wild. The problem is that in cultivating for their palates they left many of the more powerful nutrients behind. Over time these powerful components have evolved further and further out of the typical human diet.

Additionally, most of the produce available today is grown, harvested and distributed by large scale industrial systems, raised in depleted, nutrient deficient soil and carefully cultivated for long distance transportation and extended shelf life. Suffice it to say that much of the produce currently available in our country's food supply is nutritionally compromised. The dramatic rise in health issues such as cancer, obesity, adult and childhood diabetes, metabolic diseases, immunity and neurological disorders in the last half century appear as evidence of this phenomenon.

The intent of Robinson's book is not to decry the current state of things, thankfully, but to provide practical knowledge and simple tips for navigating through these issues. It's not about striking out into the woods with your gathering basket either. It's about learning what you can easily grow for yourself or find in the supermarket, what varieties to look for, how to shop for freshness, how to prepare and store all of the best produce that is widely available so you can get the most bang for your buck (and bite!).

Some good tips from *Eating on the Wild Side*:[24]

1. Tearing romaine and iceberg lettuce the day before you eat it quadruples its antioxidant content.
2. The healing properties of garlic can be maximized by slicing, chopping, mashing, or pressing it and then letting it rest for a full 10 minutes before cooking.
3. The yellowest corn in the store has 35 times more beta-carotene than white corn.
4. Cooking potatoes and then chilling them for about 24 hours before you eat them (even if you reheat them) turns a high-glycemic vegetable into a low-or moderate-glycemic vegetable. Paradoxically, combining potatoes with oil (French fry alert!) helps keep them from disrupting your metabolism.
5. Carrots are more nutritious cooked than raw. When cooked whole, they have 25 percent more falcarinol, a cancer-fighting compound, than carrots that have been sectioned before cooking.
6. Beet greens are more nutritious than the beets themselves.
7. The smaller the tomato, the more nutrients it contains. Deep red tomatoes have more antioxidants than yellow, gold, or green tomatoes.
8. The most nutritious tomatoes in the supermarket are not in the produce aisles— they are in the canned goods section! Processed tomatoes, whether

canned or cooked into a paste or sauce, are the richest known source of lycopene. They also have the most flavor.

9. Storing broccoli wrapped in a plastic bag with tiny pin pricks in it will give you up to 125 percent more antioxidants than if you had stored the broccoli loosely wrapped or in a tightly sealed bag.
10. Canned or jarred artichokes are just as nutritious as fresh.
11. Thawing frozen berries in the microwave preserves twice as many antioxidants and more vitamin C than thawing them on the counter or inside your refrigerator.
12. Ounce per ounce, there is more fiber in raspberries than in bran cereals.

Foraging

Another way to "eat wild" is to learn what's right outside your door, all for the taking. If you have a yard it's likely there's s a gold mine out there—a feast of delicious, accessible superfoods and powerful healing agents. I realize that picking things to eat out of the grass is a strange notion, especially since there are things there you should definitely NOT be consuming, but here are five that you can easily identify and probably already know. You most likely have at least one or more of them. Consider this a primer in very basic foraging.

Before I go any further, however, I need to make three things very clear. First, DO NOT consume anything that you can't *positively 100% identify*. Second, don't consume anything that has been treated with any herbicides or fertilizers. *Avoid foraging in any area that has been treated with any chemicals in the last five years.* Finally, *use common sense.* Don't collect from areas where your pets roam or along places of high pollution, such as parking lots, roadsides, etc. Soak your forage in a bowl of water with a couple of tablespoons of apple cider vinegar and rinse well before eating.

We aren't herbalists, doctors or nutritionists, therefore we are not authorities on the subject, but these are a few wild plants that we use and enjoy. There are many great resources on wild foods and herbs, so please do your own research and decide which foraged foods are right for you. With that understood, let's begin gathering the wild things!*

---

*Statements in this book have not been evaluated by the Food and Drug Administration and are not to be considered as medical or nutritional advice. This information is not intended to diagnose, treat, cure or prevent any disease, nor should it be considered above the advice of your physician. If you are pregnant or breastfeeding, consult your physician before ingesting any wild foods. Consume wild and foraged plants at your own risk. As with any food you have not previously consumed, proceed cautiously in case of allergic or other adverse reactions.

Field Guide: Edible Weeds

1. Dandelion (Taraxacum)

Everybody knows this one. From our childhood delight in blowing the fairy-like seeds into the wind, to the gardener's disdain at their seemingly endless proliferation, the dandelion is an icon of our experience with the outdoors. But little do we know how much it deserves our respect and protection!

We love the dandelion greens in salad. One serving provides more than the daily requirement of vitamins A and K. It's also high in calcium, potassium, iron, magnesium and zinc. All you have to do is pick a few, rinse, and toss them in your salad. They can also be sautéed, roasted, or baked. The roots are fantastic for a tea or coffee substitute and a tincture that has long been used to detoxify the liver and kidneys, reduce swelling and fevers, and prevent diabetes. The flowers can be used for making things like syrup, jams, and a delicious wine, traditionally consumed as a health tonic. This list is just a beginning. Here's a great link with many other ideas[25] for using the dandelion.

2. Creeping Charlie (Glechoma hederacea)

This is the low growing ivy that you see running rampant through your lawns and flower beds, NOT the house plant by the same name. Now you don't have to worry about how to get rid of it. Let it grow! Loaded with vitamin C, the young greens can be steeped into a nutritious tea. *Avoid consuming if you are pregnant or breastfeeding.*

3. Plantain (Plantago Major)

It grows almost everywhere and has an amazing number of uses. Not only is the leaf tasty and extremely nutritious, but it can also be used as an anti-inflammatory, a poultice to treat bee stings, dermatitis, insect bites and sunburn. It can stop the bleeding and accelerate the healing of wounds. It's truly like an entire medicine kit in a leaf, and the amazing thing is you can almost always find it when needed. Once you identified this gem of a plant, you'll realize how familiar it is and can start using it.

4. Chickweed (Stellaria)

Chickweed, also called starweed, is a sweet little low-growing plant with many trace minerals and nutrients. It's delicious eaten raw as an addition to any salad, very crunchy and refreshing. When eaten fresh, always begin slowly in case of allergic reaction. It also has several medicinal uses: as a healing poultice to any wound or skin irritation, a moistening agent for dry coughs or asthma, an anti-inflammatory and a diuretic. It appears most abundantly in the spring, but will come back in the fall.

The Lady Farmer Guide to Slow Living

5. Garlic Mustard (Alliaria petiolata)

Garlic Mustard is a biennial (lives for two years) that spreads through damp and disturbed locations such as roadsides and ditches. In many areas it has been labeled as an invasive weed because of its tendency to interfere with the growth of some native plants. So if you have it in your yard, don't spray it. Eat it! Garlic Mustard leaves can be used like any salad green and have a slightly peppery garlic taste. The flowers can be chopped and eaten in a salad as well. It has many health benefits such as high vitamin A and C, as well as vitamins E and B, Omega-3 fatty acids, potassium, calcium and magnesium. Check out the

Garlic Mustard Pesto recipe on the Edible Wild Food Blog.[26] This is a great website for more information on all of the plants mentioned in this section.[27] (Note; Garlic mustard contains trace amounts of cyanide, which may be reduced by soaking or blanching.)

This is just a glimpse into the world of wild and wonderful plants that are beneficial, plentiful and free! Remember, DO NOT consume anything that a) you can't positively identify; b) has been treated with any herbicides or fertilizers; or c) might be contaminated by pollution or pets.

Slow Food is Live Food

Fermentation Basics

Food preservation is key to human survival and has been for many thousands of years. Crops grown in season have to be consumed immediately or processed for year-round sustenance. That need is the same as it has always been, but in the modern world we don't have to think about it much. Less than a century ago, it was common for an American household to grow and preserve their own food, but in our current system the food industry has taken this chore mostly out of our hands. Just as the planting, cultivation and harvesting of our food takes place far out of our sight, so does the processing, preserving and packaging. In this paradigm, our first interface with one of our most fundamental daily needs is in the supermarket.

Home food preservation for most of us is a choice rather than a matter of survival, which is why the practice has declined dramatically in the past two generations. I grew up in the sixties and knew lots of people who not only ate year round from their gardens but also had plenty to share. A jar of green beans, homemade vegetable soup or pickles often showed up as a gift during the holidays or throughout the winter, reminding us of the glories of the summer harvest. In the eighties and nineties, however, the lifestyle of a typical family (including ours) didn't allow for the time, space and effort that it took to grow and process your own food. At the most it was a small-scale hobby but not a necessity.

In the last couple of decades, however, with interest in food sourcing and quality on the rise combined with the declining health of a population subsisting on commercially-processed foods, home preservation is enjoying a revival. An abundance of how-to information in print and on the internet makes it easier for even the least experienced to embrace this fun and satisfying aspect of slow living.

The most familiar home preservation techniques today are freezing, canning and drying. Another is fermentation, which is possibly the oldest way of preserving food in human history. It's different from the other methods in that instead of using techniques to keep bacteria *out* of food, it *encourages* the growth of healthy bacteria. Fermented foods are loaded with nutrients and the beneficial bacteria our bodies need for digestion and immunity, thus not only preventing spoilage but actually enhancing the nutritional value of many foods.

Although we do some canning, freezing and dehydrating of our own garden produce and what we can get close to home, we're particularly excited about fermentation here on our little homestead because it's quick, easy and doesn't involve any set-up or special equipment.

Essentially, fermentation is the process of proliferating the healthful and beneficial bacteria (probiotics) already present in and around the food, not only preserving it but also making it more nutritious and flavorful. We are surrounded by billions and trillions of microscopic organisms all around us, on and inside us. It's common in our culture to associate bacteria with lack of cleanliness and illness, but the truth is that only a tiny percentage of these organisms are harmful. The rest are our allies in living a healthful life. A broad spectrum of these microorganisms within our bodies, in our food, soil and our surrounding environment help our immune systems to grow and thrive.

Modern medical research is now confirming what has been known for many thousands of years, that fermented foods are safe and good for us! A diet including a diversity of probiotics encourages disease resistance. The overuse of multiple antibiotics in recent decades has caused an increase in organisms that are resistant to existing drugs. Consuming a broad range of probiotics not only increases our immunological defenses but increases the bioavailability of the nutrients in the foods as well. Although probiotics are widely available in the form of pills and tablets, a much greater diversity of live cultures are present in a variety of foods (without the cost, the plastic containers and the factory middleman).

Many fermented foods are already familiar to most of us. Cheese, wine, vinegar, yogurt, beer, cider, sauerkraut (the traditional kind), miso, soy sauce, kefir, etc. are all items that are readily available in most food outlets. It's important to note, however, that when a food is packaged and processed for mass distribution the probiotics are usually greatly reduced or eliminated completely. With few exceptions, self-prepared probiotic foods are far superior to anything you can buy. Following a few simple guidelines, you can create your own superfoods at home!

KEFIR

One of our favorite fermented foods here in our house is kefir! It's the superfood you need to know about, a rich, creamy probiotic beverage with the consistency of drinkable yogurt but with many times more nutrients. If you haven't discovered it yet, then read on. You're in for a treat!

Kefir is an easy, affordable and delicious way of boosting your immune system. Besides being packed with nutrients, it's a powerhouse of probiotics. These are the *good* organisms that are essential to our health, the ones that help us fight off dangerous infections. They proliferate everywhere inside our bodies and in the world around us. But with the widespread use of antibiotics, hand sanitizers and a multitude of other practices meant to keep us healthy by reducing harmful bacteria, we've actually been removing many of the body's own best defenses and have created a widespread health problem. Because antibiotics and disinfectants work against both the good and the bad bacteria, the natural balance of our microscopic universe is disrupted and we become vulnerable to resistant strains, commonly known as "superbugs."

We can help our systems restore this balance by including any probiotic rich foods in our diet, but kefir is an A+ source, containing multiple strains of live cultures and substantial amounts of protein, calcium and magnesium as well. Although it's been around for a long time, thought to have originated in the Caucasus Mountains many centuries ago, kefir has recently attracted scientific interest for its potential as a beneficial probiotic food. An article from *Frontiers in Microbiology* published in 2016 states:

> *Kefir is a complex fermented dairy product created through the symbiotic fermentation of milk by lactic acid bacteria and yeasts ... As with other fermented dairy products, kefir has been associated with a range of health benefits such as cholesterol metabolism and angiotensin-converting enzyme*

(ACE) inhibition, antimicrobial activity, tumor suppression, increased speed of wound healing, and modulation of the immune system including the alleviation of allergy and asthma ... One of the features that distinguish kefir from many other fermented dairy products is the requirement for the presence of a kefir grain in fermentation and the presence and importance of a large population of yeasts.

It is in the traditional method of making kefir, the use of the "grains" as a culture, that the diversity and abundance of probiotics can proliferate, which the article[28] goes on to explain is not the same as the widely distributed commercial product.

Commercial, industrial-scale production rarely utilizes kefir grains for fermentation, but rather uses starter cultures of microbes that have been isolated from kefir or kefir grains in order to provide more consistent products (Assadi et al., 2000). While this industrially produced kefir may have health benefits of its own, research examining such benefits has either not been performed or is not published.

In other words, the scientific community is looking at the traditionally prepared version of kefir as opposed to what you'd buy in the store. Even the store-bought brands have more live cultures than yogurt, but the probiotics really increase when you make your kefir at home. It's simple and quick.

Recipe: Homemade Kefir

1. Obtain your kefir grains (which aren't really grains at all, but small, gelatinous culture clusters that resemble tapioca). The best way is to get them fresh from someone who makes it on a regular basis, but there are also

multiple online sources. You can also get kefir starters, but you want the live grains for the more nutritionally potent, traditionally prepared kefir. Grains should be stored (while not being used) in cow's milk – in between uses or when you have extra. You'll want to refresh this milk (about weekly) to keep the grains fed and happy.

2. Place about ¼ cup of live kefir culture grains in 1/2 gallon of cow or goat milk.

3. Cover with a cloth secured by a rubber band or a loosely turned lid and place in a warm spot out of direct sunlight until it's the consistency of liquid yogurt. Fermentation times will differ based on a multitude of variables, especially temperature. In summer it takes 24 hours or less in our kitchen. In winter it can take up to two days before it thickens.

4. Strain the grains from the kefir using a plastic strainer over a bowl or large measuring cup (I use the ½-gallon Pyrex) and a wooden spoon to stir it through until most of the liquid is strained into the bowl and only the grains remain in the strainer. Place the grains in a jar of fresh milk and store in the refrigerator for future use.

5. At this point you now have your kefir in the bowl and can flavor it any number of ways. For starters, try 1/2 cup of fruit, the juice of one lemon, or a tablespoon of vanilla or almond extract, sweeten with sugar, honey, maple syrup or stevia. Your imagination is the limit here. Experiment and have fun with it.

6. Use a hand blender to smooth it out, leave at room temperature for another 4-6 hours for its "second ferment" (this step increases the probiotic content but is optional), then chill. I think the flavors are optimal when it's cold.

7. Now drink and enjoy and know you are doing yourself and your health a huge favor!

FERMENTED VEGETABLES

Fermented vegetables are not only an easy way to get your probiotics, but also a quick way to preserve fresh produce with minimal fuss. Although the foods need refrigeration once they are prepared and last several months as opposed to the year or more with canned goods, the simplicity of this process has us hooked!

The only equipment you need other than the vegetables, a chopping board and a good knife are salt, water and jars with lids.

Almost any vegetable or combination of several can be cultured. Basically you just cut it up and put it in a jar with a brine (salt water), leave it for a few days until it ferments to your taste. One of my favorite go-to sites for fermenting is *Cultured Food Life* by Donna Schwenk.[29] She has an entire section on fermenting vegetables here. Another great resource is Sandor Katz's classic book *Wild Fermentation*.[30] Check these out and try a few of these recipes. Once you get the idea, you can start experimenting and come up with your own favorite combinations of vegetables and flavorings. One of our favorites is this slaw recipe below.

Recipe: Probiotic Summer Slaw

We got several big, beautiful heads of purple cabbage out of the garden this year. Planted in the spring or fall months, it's easy to grow and packed with vitamins, minerals, fiber, and antioxidants. Plus it will keep for a good while if stored in a cool place, so it's well worth the space it takes to grow. Cabbage is a great vegetable to ferment as well, which enhances the level of nutrients and turns it into a probiotic powerhouse! Here's our method for making a fermented slaw, a variation of sauerkraut that's ready to eat in a few days' time.

Makes 3 half gallon jars of fermented slaw

- 3 medium to large heads of purple cabbage
- 9 medium to large carrots
- 3 medium onions
- 3 cloves of garlic
- 1 bunch of celery
- 1 handful of fresh parsley
- Sea Salt (to taste)*
- 6 fresh grape or oak leaves

1. In a food processor, chop all of the ingredients to a texture that is somewhat fine but still has a good crunch to it. We did this in batches, one head of cabbage and 1/3 of the other ingredients at a time.
2. Place the processed vegetable blend into a large bowl and add plenty of salt to taste. Stir well and let it sit for a few minutes. The salt will draw the moisture out of the cabbage.
3. Once the mixture is well moistened, begin spooning it into one of the half gallon mason jars, packing it tightly until about two inches from the top.
4. Add just enough water to cover.
5. Take 2 grape or oak leaves and one at a time, press them down firmly over the top of the vegetables. Add water if needed until entire contents are covered by a half inch or so.

6. Place the lid tightly on the jar and put it on a shelf or counter at room temperature out of direct sunlight.
7. Let it sit for about three days, then taste it for crunch and zest. In the cooler months it might need a little more time. In the warmer months, you'll want to check it before it over-ferments and becomes mushy.
8. When you're happy with the flavor, put it in the refrigerator and enjoy! It will stay good for several weeks in the fridge, but you'll love it so much it probably won't last that long.

*The proper amount of salt takes some practice. You want to get enough for proper fermentation, so begin with adding until the taste is a little bit *too* salty. It will mellow as it ferments. If it remains too salty to eat, it's not wasted. You can use it to mix in soup! Then next time you can cut back until you discover the right amount for your taste, the salt you are using, the bacteria in your environment, etc.

Mary E. Kingsley

SOURDOUGH

Sourdough is a fermentation (called a "starter") that when added to bread dough, allows it to rise naturally. Its use as a leavening agent for baking probably goes back as far as the beginnings of agriculture. The bacteria in sourdough (lactobacilli) actually help to break down or "predigest" the proteins (including gluten) in the flour, making the nutrients more bioavailable in the body. Some people (but not all) who have experienced digestive problems with the wheat in commercially produced bread might be able to tolerate sourdough. The fermentation process also makes the bread more nutritious, particularly in B vitamins, and lowers its glycemic effects (the degree to which it raises blood sugar).

You will need sourdough starter to use in bread recipes instead of commercial yeast. You can either get it from somewhere else, such as a bread baking friend or an internet source—or you can make it yourself fairly easily. Here are some resources:

1. "How To Obtain or Make a Sourdough Starter." *Cultures for Health Lactofermented Hummus Comments*, 31 Jan. 2018, https://www.culturesforhealth.com/learn/sourdough/how-to-obtain-sourdough-starter/.
2. Donna's Live Sourdough Culture (Product) https://www.culturedfoodlife.com/store/product/donnas-sourdough-culture/

We got our own sourdough starter several years ago from a neighbor whose mother had started it fifteen years before that. Since then we've passed it along to others who in turn share it until it reaches out to the whole community and beyond. Once when ours went bad from too many days sitting out in the warm summer kitchen we were easily able to replace it through someone who originally got it from us!

Recipe: Sourdough Soda Bread

There are many sourdough bread recipes around, some of them more involved than others. Here's one that we have been enjoying lately, so quick and at least so far, fool proof. It's actually a variation on a King Arthur soda bread recipe but I've taken liberties with it according to what I have on hand, and it's been delicious every time!

Makes two 6" to 8" loaves

- 2 1/2 cups whole wheat flour or oat flour
- 1 1/4 cups all-purpose or Einkorn flour
- 1/2 cup coarsely chopped seeds and grains of your choice (chia seeds, ground walnuts, sunflower seeds, pumpkin seeds, etc.)
- 1 teaspoon baking soda
- 3/4 teaspoon salt
- 1 cup sourdough starter, ripe (fed) or discard
- 1/4 cup (4 tablespoons) melted butter
- 3 tablespoons honey
- 3/4 cup milk

1. Preheat the oven to 400°F. Lightly grease a baking sheet, or line it with parchment.
2. In a medium-sized mixing bowl, whisk together the flours, grains and seeds, baking soda, and salt.

3. In a separate bowl (or in a measuring cup), whisk together the starter, butter, honey, and milk. Pour this mixture into the dry ingredients and stir to combine. The dough will be stiff; if it's too crumbly to squeeze together, add another tablespoon or two of milk.
4. Knead the dough a couple of times to make sure it's holding together, divide it in half, and shape each half into a ball. Flatten the balls slightly, and place them on the prepared baking sheet. Use a sharp knife to cut a 1/2"-deep cross, extending all the way to the edges, atop each loaf.
5. Bake the loaves for 30 to 40 minutes, until they're golden brown and a cake tester or toothpick inserted into the center comes out clean. Remove the loaves from the oven, and brush their tops with melted butter, if desired.

Section One Reflections

1. What industrial foods do you now use that you think would be the most difficult to eliminate? Which foods that are a part of your diet now can be replaced with something that has less processing, miles traveled, packaging or ingredients?

To help you answer this, ask these questions about every item in your next meal, including animal or plant.

- What did it look like in its original form?
- How far has it traveled?
- What sort of factory, facility or human hands has it passed through to get here?
- What sort of packaging did it come in?
- How many ingredients does it contain?

2. Consider some form of gratitude practice before eating. Typically called "the blessing" or "saying grace," it can be simply taking a few seconds to acknowledge what's on your plate, where it came from and how it came to you for your nourishment.

3. Consider the "linear" versus the "circular" mindset in your most frequent food choices, including distance from the source, packaging and waste. What changes can you make in your current habits that move them in the direction of health and sustainability?

Section Two: Slow Fashion

From Seed to Sewn to Sold

"And the Lord God made for Adam and for his wife garments of skins, and clothed them."
—Genesis 3:21 RSV[31]

According to Genesis, there was a time when man didn't need clothes. Adam and Eve lived happily naked in the Garden of Eden before they ate the forbidden fruit. God was angry, but he didn't cast them out to till the land without something to wear. The Lord knew they'd be needing clothes for what was ahead!

So there we have it, the human need for the warmth and protection of garments is universal—even biblical. Aside from possibly a few remaining indigenous people and the small number of "naturists" around the world who choose nudity in specified communities (and climates!) or in their own homes, essentially everyone requires body covering on a daily basis.

Looking back to our ancient predecessors who handcrafted their own garments from the materials in their immediate surroundings, we have to be impressed by how enormously that has changed in a relatively short period of time. Nomadic hunter-gatherers used animal hides and existing vegetation, but it was the advent of agriculture some 10,000-12,000 years ago that allowed humans to grow plants and cultivate animals for woven textiles.

The earliest use of cotton, silk and linen shows up around 5,000 BC in India, Egypt and China.[32] Although textile trade across Europe, Asia and the Far East thrived in the ancient world, the goods were for mostly royalty and the upper classes. Production methods remained unchanged for several centuries until the invention of steam-powered mechanization and the sewing machine during the Industrial Revolution. Suddenly, high quality textiles were mass produced and more affordable to a much wider audience.

Textile production in America began in the late 18th century and over the next decades became the dominant industry in the country, with the establishment of hundreds of companies.[33] Textile factories thrived in this country for nearly two hundred years until changes in trade laws allowed producers to move manufacturing overseas, where cheap labor and less regulation would allow for increased profits.

This is the beginning of the phenomenon we call "fast fashion." Over the last several decades as the volume of imported, mass produced clothing has increased in the marketplace at artificially low prices, the American consumer's addiction to cheap, disposable clothing has fed and grown this toxic beast to the size of a major global crisis.

The apparel industry is a leading source of pollution on the planet. Staggering amounts of water are used to make a single t-shirt that's flown all over the globe for different stages of production before hitting some chain retail shelf for a few dollars. Many of the chemicals and dyes used to color and treat clothing are known carcinogens and hormone disrupters, directly absorbed into your bloodstream through your skin.[34] Hands that sew each individual garment belong to a person earning slave wages and working in unsafe conditions.[35]

Do we have your attention yet? The fashion industry has

crossed multiple boundaries in terms of lack of concern for people or the planet and lack of responsibility for the destructive nature of their practices. Yet the vast majority of consumers look the other way for a number of reasons—because they don't know the facts, it's too overwhelming a problem, or they don't see any alternatives.

Slow fashion is about understanding this truth and choosing another way. It's really very simple. It's about knowing where your clothes come from, what they are made of, who made them and what's in them or on them that you're breathing and wearing on your skin. It's also about what will become of them once they are no longer useful to you.

If we are to be stewards of the earth, creating a better world for ourselves and a future for our children, then we have to say "no" to this behemoth of a system. That's it. If this seems overwhelming or out of reach to you, you've come to the right place. There aren't that many choices outside the system at this point but there is so much we all can do. Coming to the realization of this situation is how Lady Farmer came to be—and we're committed to offering you slow living alternatives in this fast fashion world.

Seed: Farm to Closet

Shortly after embarking on this adventure into slow fashion, we recognized the parallels between our messaging and what we've seen happening in the food consumer world over the last decade or so. At some point people began to wake up to how our food production and distribution systems have been hijacked by giant industries, policies and politics, creating a growing disconnection between humans and the source of their daily sustenance. The result has been a widespread consumer demand for quality and transparency and the now mainstream "Farm to Table" movement. We need to see this same discernment in the apparel industry as well. With initiatives such as Fashion Revolution (#whomademyclothes),[36] The Ethical Fashion Forum,[37] and *The True Cost*[38] documentary, awareness of problems within the industry is growing.

The term "Farm to Closet" sheds light on these parallels between food and fashion and highlights the fact that clothing, like food, is an agricultural product. Cotton, flax, hemp, bamboo, jute, sisal, eucalyptus, etc. are all plants that are cultivated for fibers to be made into textiles, the basis of our clothing. Sheep and alpaca provide wool. The more we can close the transparency gap between the seed in the ground, the animals in the pasture and the clothes in our closet, the more empowered we will be to make choices that do not compromise the well-being of industry workers, the environment or ourselves.

As a consumer culture with the power to shape the marketplace, when we ask questions and insist on standards regarding our clothing as well as our food, we will begin to see changes in the industry. When we use our dollar to say "no" to practices not compatible with a healthy, humane and sustainable society, those practices will eventually disappear.

So are you ready to take a look in your closet? We hate to be the bearer of bad news, but unfortunately, unless you're already a highly conscious consumer, most of your wardrobe contains dangerous levels of toxins. It was probably manufactured using slavery and will most likely be in the landfill forever when you get rid of it, seeping those toxins back into our soil and water.

It's not a pleasant realization, but it's the truth, and as they say, the truth will set you free.

Here are a few random tidbits (linked to articles) that might make you start looking at your closet differently:

1. Your brightly colored accessories might well contain dangerous amounts of lead.[39]

2. All of those fleece jackets we love? They actually shed up to 2 grams of microfiber plastic each time we wash them,[40] sending them into our waterways and eventually into our drinking water and yes, onto our dinner plates. Got plastic?

3. Many of the chemicals used in the dying of fabrics can cause cancer and/or be disruptive to normal hormonal functioning.[41]

4. Most garments sold in the USA today are manufactured overseas, much of it produced with slave labor.[42]
5. The average American creates 82 lbs. of textile waste every year,[43] creating an annual 10.5 million tons of clothing in landfills. Most components of these textiles are full of toxic chemicals and never break down.

We don't bring these things up to send you on a guilt trip. There is an enormous lack of transparency in the current fashion industry and the vast majority of consumers really don't know the truth behind the clothes they are buying and wearing.

So what do you do? Here are some steps that will help guide all of us out of this crisis of consumer chaos into a more balanced relationship with clothing, one of our most basic human necessities.

- Decide that you want to be part of the revolution—slow fashion— and realize that big changes don't happen overnight. Paradigm shifts take time.

- Become informed! Slow fashion is a growing movement and you don't have to look far these days to learn more. We will continue to provide resources and alternatives, so keep checking in.

- Stop buying fast fashion! Bargain mega-chains have grown to monstrous proportions, fueled solely by the voracious appetites of addicted consumers demanding more and more cheap, disposable clothing. Take a hard look at your shopping habits. Use the clothes you have as long as you can, go to thrift and consignment shops, swaps and rummage sales.

- Think "Farm-to-Closet" when considering your purchases. If you don't know the type of plant or animal that's the source of the fabric, you might want to think again.

The life blood of fast fashion is your dollar ... use yours as the powerful tool that it is!

Sewn: Fabric Sourcing & Manufacturing

We started Lady Farmer with one main mission in mind: to create a line of clothes that we love and will be able to share with others, and to keep integrity at the forefront of all aspects of the supply and production chain. Our intention was to create sustainable, earth-friendly clothing from American grown and produced fabrics. Given those parameters, we quickly discovered that our options were extremely limited. With the North American Fair Trade Agreement[44] signed into law in 1994, domestic sourcing and manufacturing all but disappeared to foreign shores where cheap labor and lack of regulation resulted in the current fast fashion scenario. Couple that with the fact that the options for healthy and environmentally responsible fabrics are limited anyway and you'll get why we've been scratching our heads. With conventionally grown cotton, polyester, synthetic and antimicrobial blends, fleece, industrial fibers made from plastic bottles, a myriad of chemicals, toxic dyes, solvents all OFF our list, we've had to look carefully at our choices.

As far as textile sourcing, we've pinpointed these fabrics and materials that we're really excited about potentially using:

1. Hemp (Cannabis Sativa) is arguably top on the list of up-and-coming fabrics. In terms of sustainability, it has no equal. It grows so densely that it requires significantly less land per unit and suppresses weed growth, therefore minimizing the need for herbicides. It grows quickly and efficiently, taking less time from seed to harvest than more traditional crops and can be harvested not only for fabric but for a multitude of other uses as well (oil from the seeds can even be used as biofuel![45]). Because the roots reach so deeply into the ground, it actually aerates and supports healthy soil that is both disease and pest resistant—another way of minimizing the need for pesticides and fertilizers and enhancing its value as a cover crop. According to one source, 1 acre of hemp will produce as much fiber as that which can be grown on 2-3 acres of cotton.[46]

Hemp is nothing new. In fact it's quite old, cultivated for the last twelve millennia or so for the production of rope, canvas, paper and clothing. The first American flag was made of hemp, and now its uses have evolved into car parts, building materials, medicine, fuel and food—truly a remarkable plant. It is such a useful and viable crop that in the early days of American history a person could go to jail for *not* growing it on their land![47] So what exactly is hemp, where did it go, and why has it been against the law to grow it in this country for the better part of a century?

First of all, let's get this one scientific fact straight. *Hemp is not marijuana.* Both hemp and marijuana are plants of the species Cannabis Sativa L., but are distinct from one another in the same way that a Chihuahua and a St. Bernard are different breeds of dogs. The oilseed and fiber varieties of Cannabis are known for numerous industrial and environmental uses and do *not* have the psychogenic effect of its relative. No high with hemp![48]

Yet the two are still conflated. This guilt-by-name-association has been a most unfortunate misconception since growing marijuana was outlawed with The Marihuana Tax Act of

1937.[49] Over the next several years hemp struggled for its own identity separate from its infamous relative. The film "Hemp for Victory" was created in 1942 encouraging US farmers to grow hemp to support the war effort, but as the years went by its association with marijuana continued to strengthen through the efforts of competing interests. Then both were named in the Controlled Substances Act of 1970,[50] effectively removing one of the most useful crops in the world from the American economy. Since then China, Romania, Hungary, India and Canada have had a grand time growing it for us. Estimated annual sales for hemp products in the US are reported at more than $580 million annually.[51]

The good news is that there is now widespread recognition amongst scientists, environmentalists, farmers, and entrepreneurs that the laws are outdated and based on misinformation. It's time to bring hemp growing home. The 2014 Farm Bill allows it by permit under the auspices of a state pilot or research program. Colorado legalized it in 2014. Some states, Kentucky for example, have successfully reintroduced hemp cultivation through these permitting programs and our very own state of Maryland just passed its own hemp bill in 2018. Subsequently, the 2018 Farm Bill passed in December of that year "removes hemp from the Controlled Substances Act, places full federal regulatory authority of hemp with USDA, and allows State departments of agriculture to file hemp programs plans and regulate hemp cultivation per their State specific programs."[52]

Although it will take some time for the new laws and regulations to go into effect, commercial hemp cultivation is on the very precipice of coming back to the US. This is a major step in the direction of a domestically grown and manufactured textile compatible with the highest of health and environmental standards. Furthermore, growing our own hemp and overseeing the processing and manufacturing of the fabric is a goal for us at Lady Farmer, as it would give us the opportunity for absolute transparency every step of the way.

2. Linen comes from the fibers of the flax plant. It is one of the oldest fabrics used on the planet, proof of its use dating nearly 10,000 years, going back to the beginnings of civilization along the fertile crescent in Egypt, the Dead Sea and later on in many areas of BC-era Europe. It has a special place in American pioneer history, as many homesteaders had their own patch of flax which would be hand processed, spun into fiber and woven into cloth. Linen became less economical to produce as the textile industry began to emerge and was surpassed by cotton after the invention of the cotton gin in the late 18th century, therefore becoming more expensive and less accessible to the not-so-wealthy. With new technologies, however, simplifying the production and processing of flax, it has enjoyed a renaissance in recent years as an affordable and fashionable choice in fabrics. Because it is 100% natural, it's completely biodegradable. We love it for its beauty, versatility and simplicity—all the reasons that it's endured for thousands of years as staple in clothing production in many parts of the world.

3. Lyocell—a lovely discovery! For those of you who aren't familiar with Tencel (the brand name for Lyocell, from the European Company Lenzing), it is incredibly soft and light but also weighty and smooth, and drapes in all the right ways. While man-made, it is sustainably produced using a "closed-loop" system, meaning it uses minimal resources and has little to no waste. You can read more about the process on the Tencel website[53] or a quick Google search will lead you to other third party sources that talk about Lyocell. Even though it is technically a synthetic fabric, it is made with all-natural materials in a low-impact manner that makes it completely biodegradable! This may be our favorite thing about it.

4. Organic Cotton. There's a lot of misinformation about cotton fabrics. The industry does a brilliant job of marketing this product as "natural" and healthy, the stuff of baby blankets and carefree summer dresses, "the fabric of our lives™,"[54] etc. The reality is that conventionally grown cotton, which makes up 50% of the world's fiber production by producing 29 million tons annually,[55] is a resource intensive and toxic crop. It uses 3% of the world's arable land and is responsible for 3% of the global water footprint[56] as well as more than 10% of all the world's pesticide use.[57] That's why at Lady Farmer we are committed to using *only organically grown* cotton in our products. The organic cotton market currently represents only a very small percentage of global cotton production, but with education and increasing consumer awareness, the hope is that the market will eventually dictate more responsible practices in the larger industry.

5. Wool. Lady Farmer is looking forward to collaborating with climate beneficial wool producers in the next year to source for our up-and-coming knit apparel. These producers work with soil scientists in grazing and flock management, maximizing the carbon sequestration that occurs naturally in non-industrial ruminate farming. Fibershed[58] is an organization that "develops regional and regenerative fiber systems on behalf of independent working producers, by expanding opportunities to implement carbon farming, forming catalytic foundations to rebuild regional manufacturing, and through connecting end-users to farms and ranches through public education. We envision the emergence of an international system of regional textile communities that enliven connection and ownership of 'soil-to-soil' textile processes." These regional textile communities supported by Fibershed reinforce the emphasis on local sourcing outside of the prevalent industry, embraced by Lady Farmer and other sustainably-minded initiatives as the ideal in reinventing the current apparel production paradigm.

Our position on fabrics using recycled materials (such as plastic water bottles, for example) is to avoid using them as much as possible. Processing and manufacturing of these products are resource intensive and actually do very little to reduce the waste problems that they claim to be addressing. One of the dangers of these industries is the public perception that it's okay to continue the use of things like plastic water bottles and other single use plastics because someone is going to take care of it afterwards. Recycling as a whole is not the answer to our waste problems on the planet. It's much more about consumer choice. As for the prevalence of athletic wear and fleece, there has been a heightened awareness in the last year of the damaging microfibers present in these fabrics. The tiny shreds of plastic are released into the water system through the laundry and eventually end up in the ocean, where they are consumed by marine life and end up on our plates and in our bodies. Fortunately, this has gotten the public's attention to some degree.[59]

While the path to our production goals might be narrow, it is at least clear. We don't have much choice in American grown sustainable fabrics at this time, so we do the best we can. So far we have been able to locate responsibly manufactured organic cotton, Tencel, linen and hemp from reliable sources. However, much of it is grown in China, which brings us to where we are today.

Sold: A Good Price

What do we think when we say something is "a good price"? We usually take it to mean an item can be bought for less than its actual worth. In other words, it's good for the *consumer*, who enjoys a net gain on a particular item. It's an incentive, the driving force in our acquisition economy, empowering the buyer to always be seeking more. It's exciting! Picture the throngs of shoppers pouring into the marketplace on Black Friday, answering the beacon call of the deep discount: CLEARANCE! PRICES SLASHED! BLOW OUT SALE!

This is what we might call "past paradigm" thinking, the fundamental assumption that we are entitled to as much as we can get for the least amount of money. Pause and think about this for a moment. Is this not ingrained in all of us to some degree? Isn't bargain shopping a good thing, a smart thing, often a form of harmless entertainment? Isn't it true in the world as we know it?

The problem is that this fundamental assumption, accepted as truth in our society, is supporting an unsustainable system that must change for us to move towards healing.

Here's something to consider: What if "a good price" meant that the cost of the item actually reflected its true value all the way down the line, from the seller to the manufacturer to the supply chain to the producer of the raw materials? What if "a good price" meant a decent wage for every human being involved in the production and the enforcement of responsible environmental and health standards?

Mary E. Kingsley

What if we all thought of these things when looking at a price tag with the goal not being to spend as little as possible, but to exchange our own resources for something with meaning and integrity?

Consumers have confronted this issue over the last several years in the context of the organic/local food movement. The fact is that "real" food costs more—and with the emergence of neighborhood farmers' markets and local food sourcing, shoppers are given a clear choice of quality over cost. Hopefully the public is beginning to understand that as a basic daily necessity, good food is worth the extra cost and the reasons for it are valid. Our perception that the main goal of producers is to present us with the cheapest possible product is hopefully shifting with a deeper understanding of sourcing, supply chains, and the need for transparency all along the way.

This evolution in the food industry has paved the way for a similar shift in fashion. Increasingly over the last several decades consumers have come to expect a deal on every article of clothing, the cheaper the better. To that end producers have cut costs and wages and environmental safeguards to shreds all across the globe. No matter where it is from, how it was made or what toxin a garment is dyed with or dipped in, the American public has demonstrated that low cost and quantity, not quality, is the fuel for its voracious consumption. We demand rock bottom prices on fashion, while the ones paying the true costs of all of this dirt cheap clothing are exploited workers and a polluted planet. What results is an enormously wasteful throw-away clothing culture. The clothes cost less and therefore are valued less and thoughtlessly disposed of to an astonishing degree.

As a company, Lady Farmer designs and produces a sustainable alternative to the mass-produced commodities that are pervasive in today's fashion industry. Our clothing reflects the highest standards of environmental sustainability, health considerations and fair labor practices. We also seek to provide the knowledge needed to make informed decisions about clothing because when more consumers are aware and are demanding more from producers (brands), the paradigm will shift towards a healthier system that benefits everyone.

As it is, higher quality and ethically produced goods will cost more than Americans have been accustomed to paying—but there are other ways to refuse buying into this wasteful system. This is an ongoing discussion in our community.

Secondhand clothing is a great choice. Thrift and consignment stores, clothing swaps, wardrobe repair and "upcycling" are all ways of rejecting the prevailing system with minimal cost. Merely increasing awareness of personal lifestyle and consumer habits are powerful tools as well. Individuals can quickly learn that a sense of well-being is not necessarily compromised by consuming less, but can in fact be enhanced by such reevaluation. We support and encourage all of these efforts.

For those seeking the option of new, sustainably-produced clothing, however, our goal is to offer fashionable, multi-functional garments that will fit your life for many seasons and years to come. Be assured that the price tag on each of our garments is a truly "good price," good for everyone down the line, reflecting the care and well-being of all involved in bringing these pieces to you—from seed to sewn to sold.

Section Two Reflections

1. When did you first become aware of problems within the fast fashion industry?

2. How has your awareness changed your habits, both in your shopping and in what you wear?

3. How has this awareness affected other areas of your life?

4. Do you have too many clothes? What happens when you try to get rid of some of them? Reflect on your answer and ask yourself if that tendency can be seen in other parts of your life as well?

5. What are your thoughts about "a good price?" It's an interesting exercise because this is a place where people often get defensive. Try to remove any feelings of judgment or justification and simply observe what feelings come up around this question.

Section Three: Slow Spaces

Shelter

"One had to build shelters. One had to make pockets and live inside them."

—Lorrie Moore[60]

"Don't own so much clutter that you will be relieved to see your house catch fire."

—Wendell Berry[61]

Since the very beginning, humans have sought shelter from the wild. From trees and caves and mud huts to cabins and castles, condos, mansions, tiny houses—each era in history and place on the planet offers its own version of the ideal dwelling place. Yet from Lincoln's log cabin to Buckingham Palace the purpose is the same—to provide a space of protection and comfort for the inhabitants.

Once again, we don't have to look very far to see that living trends seem to be constantly evolving. In just the last century there has been significant movement back and forth from rural to urban and suburban areas, from the farm to the city to the subdivision. Since the invention of the automobile and the widespread availability of an immediate food supply, geography is not the limitation that it once was even a couple of generations back. The deciding factor in our current society is much more likely to be economics. People are no longer following the source of their food, but employment and affordability.

So what does that mean for us as we explore the idea of slow living and the search for a deeper connection to the source of our well-being? There's a great deal of frustration about where and how we live in our society. The "normal" pace of life often feels like struggle and depletion. The perceived "ideal" situation feels unobtainable, unaffordable, out of reach due to circumstances such as a job, family obligations, or any number of limiting factors. Institutions and industries have more say about where we live than our hearts' desires. In other words, we may feel our lives are running *us* and not the other way around.

I think many of us can relate. There might be times in our lives when our living situations make us feel like a fish out of water, even though it might have been the *right* thing for many reasons. We feel impatient to have the setting we want, to get on to our dream place, or at least something closer to it. If you live with a yearning that wants to take you away from the miracle of your here and now, or an ache that makes the life you have in mind for yourself seem perpetually beyond your grasp, let me say this. No matter where or how you live, you can have what you want at any moment.

"And how is that?" you ask. "I can't afford that house, or make the changes necessary to move to a farm or the town or location of my dreams to live the lifestyle that provides everything that is missing from the one I have now, that way of being that is calling to me every single day."

Here's how. It's really quite simple. What you are longing for is not a place at all. It's a feeling. The feeling is all we ever want. Where we get all mixed up is in thinking we need a certain thing or situation to have it, but it's not true. A feeling is just that, and it's not a result of our circumstances or surroundings—but in how we perceive ourselves and those things that make up our lives.

Think about that, but keep reading because here's the *real* thing: the more you practice creating the *feeling* of where and how you want to live, the closer you actually move towards that reality. If that sounds like a miracle—it is. I can't tell you *how* it works, I can only tell you that it does.

The purpose of this section of the book is to help you live your slow living life in your current space—*one moment at a time*. It doesn't require a lot of money, time, or at least initially even an address or job change. What it does require is a willingness to tune in to your surroundings, learn to discern what is agitating or discomforting, and choose what is soothing, nurturing and restorative. Learn what moves you in the direction of that magical feeling that will get you where you want to be.

Surroundings

The very first step in effecting change in our lives pursuant to our spaces is to recognize that our immediate surroundings influence us greatly in both conscious and unconscious ways. When we develop enough self-awareness to notice our own ill feelings in a situation, be it discomfort, agitation or anxiety, instead of blaming ourselves or our lives for our general malaise, we can perhaps look around and realize what in our surroundings is not supporting our well-being. Conversely, when we feel lighthearted, comfortable, relaxed and peaceful—it's useful to notice where we are and assess how our environment is lifting our spirits.

For example, notice how you feel when you are in a room with no windows, or in a cozy coffee shop, on the beach or walking through a wooded landscape. Despite what we perceive to be our dominant life circumstances, our immediate surroundings can have a huge effect on how we feel at any given time.

If we are affected to such a degree by our surroundings, then our living spaces where we eat, sleep, wake and keep our belongings should be a major contributor to our general sense of well-being or lack of it. We are not so disconnected from our environment as to be unsusceptible to clutter, chaos or uncleanliness. When we become aware of how our lives are impacted by the physical things and spaces around us, then we have the power to change whatever it is that doesn't serve our health and happiness. Read on.

STUFF

I have this memory from back in the '80's, when as a young married couple my husband and I were making a move across several states. We'd spent hours and hours packing up our apartment and loading it all onto a truck. Standing on the curb as it finally pulled away, exhausted and sweating (it was summer in New Orleans), my friend made the wry remark, "With any luck you'll never see it again."

It was a joke, of course, but the deeper truth of it struck me at the time and I've never forgotten it. They were valued items, to be sure, all those gifts our loved ones had chosen from our "registry" for us to begin our lives together and the things we'd collected for our household as newlyweds, certainly worth the time, money and energy we'd expended to own them, use them and now move them several hundred miles. Weren't they? Those were all things we *needed*.

Yet I knew there was absolutely nothing on that truck we couldn't have lived without or easily replaced, including all the wedding china, the fondue set, the blender, the sheet sets and framed posters.

Thirty years later and counting I look at my surroundings and ask, is the sentimental value of it all held in this or that object, or in our hearts as memories and experience? In other words, what do we do with all of the STUFF!

By now, most people are aware of clutter as a problem and we all must deal with it to some degree. For decades we've been getting advice from the experts on how to manage the constant flood of objects into our living spaces, what to toss, what to keep and how to manage it. From Don Aslett's *Clutter's Last Stand*[52] in the '80's followed by organization guru Julie Morgenstern with *Organizing From the Inside Out*[63] and more recently the phenomenon of Marie Kondo and *The Life-Changing Magic of Tidying Up*,[64] we've been inundated with all manner of methods, philosophies and rituals for keeping our heads above this rising tide of material items in our midst.

Unlike other living creatures on the planet, humans seem to be unique in the need for "things" to help us in almost every aspect of our existence. We can probably chalk it up to the fact that our brains are evolved enough to create solutions for everything that presents itself as a problem or challenge (for example—the spear for obtaining food, baskets for gathering, tools for building and agriculture, the wheel for moving heavy things, etc.). Such innovations were undoubtedly necessary for the survival of the species and continued to be for thousands of years. The rising demands of our increasingly complex cultures, however, necessitated more and more "things" and eventually outpaced the old methods of making these essentials, giving rise to new systems. Thus, around two hundred years ago, civilization took a path of no return, entering an era of unprecedented societal change known as the Industrial Revolution. Mass production of cheap goods became the driving force behind economic growth and defined our way of life like nothing before.

From this point until the present time, almost anything and everything can be made quickly, cheaply and in enormous quantities. Driven by the messages of a consumer/cash economy, our concept of what's "necessary" has grown exponentially with every passing year until our living spaces can no longer hold it all. That's why the self-storage industry was expected to rise to a value of $37.5 billion in 2017[65] and the demand for home organization products is expected to rise to $10.5 billion by the end of 2019.[66]

What's even more concerning is that for most of the past century, an increasing amount of this "stuff" being produced is either made entirely of plastic or at least contains plastic parts. Unlike our bodies when we die and natural objects produced by earlier humans, the earth can't absorb these synthetic things when their useful lives are over. For those of us trying to simplify and declutter our living spaces, the knowledge that getting things out of our sight doesn't eliminate them from being a problem somewhere else only makes our task more difficult.

Indeed, we have come full circle. We find ourselves asking the question, what is the slow living solution for our "solutions?" When almost every product we use in our daily lives is either made of or enshrouded in plastic, when there are no effective systems for dealing with these permanent waste materials (recycling is limited, at best), when our efforts to choose/request sustainable materials for everyday uses are thwarted, when our longing for peace and simplicity in our living spaces conflicts with culture, family, time, etc.—*what can we do?*

Dealing with our clutter is a journey. It takes self-awareness to recognize the problems that it creates in our lives and then time, energy and determination to actually do something about it. Unless it's something that's ingrained in our daily habits, it becomes the thing to do "later," which often becomes much later or never. In the meantime the problems get worse. The solution is to get started.

So, we take a deep breath and recognize that this is not something that will be solved overnight. As with most tasks that seem enormous or even impossible, we take a simple approach. Start small. Do what you can. Avoid judgment of yourself and others.

Product Clutter

Have you ever stopped to wonder why is it that there are so many different household products for a few basic needs? And furthermore, why is it that almost 100% of those products are consumable (cooking, cleaning and personal hygiene supplies, etc.) but at least some if not all of their packaging is permanent and indestructible? How many of these products have only one use, or are consumed over a short period of time, leaving the legacy of their clamshells or cellophane wrappers for thousands of years? Our planet is overflowing with billions of tons of packaging refuse that literally has nowhere to go but our oceans and landfills. What's more, this whole phenomenon is still so recent in our society that we have yet to realize how these chemically compounded substances will affect us as they leach into our soil and water. This is nothing less than tragic for our earth and every being living on it.

As a positive step, we can flip the "multiple products per need" paradigm around to "products with multiple uses." This not only addresses the over-use of plastics and packaging, but can also drastically reduce home clutter (and expense!) as well.

To see results quickly, start under the sink in the kitchen, bathroom and laundry. In our house we had some definite goals that made the decisions about what to eliminate a lot easier.

1. Replace any single-use items with natural, multi-use household products
2. Reduce plastic containers by switching to glass whenever possible
3. Replace products containing toxic chemicals with natural and/or DIY products

These are just a few of the very common and inexpensive household products that will take you a long way towards decluttering and reducing packaging and toxins. They can be used alone or in combination for dozens of product replacements and a multitude of purposes.

- Vinegar
- Baking soda
- Lemons
- Citric acid
- Epsom salts
- Essential oils, etc.

Here is a partial list of their uses in these areas:

IN THE KITCHEN:

- Surface cleaner—half vinegar/half water in a spray bottle. For a fresh fragrance, keep a quart jar 2/3 full of vinegar and add leftover citrus peels when you have them. Refill your spray bottle from the jar as needed.

- Disinfectant—use a few drops of essential lemon or lime oil around the sink faucet, under the backsplash and other areas where water tends to collect
- Pot and pan scrub—baking soda mixed with water or vinegar to make a light abrasive paste.
- Rinse-Aid— 1/2 cup of vinegar added to your dishwasher load (don't put it in the little compartment, it might corrode the parts). For extra clean and sparkle, add 1/4 cup of citric acid as well.
- Half a lemon cut into half again and tossed into your garbage disposal will freshen your drain.

In the laundry:

- In place of laundry detergent, use 1/4 cup of baking soda dissolved in the washer before adding clothes.
- Add a 1/2 cup of vinegar to the wash for extra cleaning power.
- Add lemon juice to the rinse cycle for freshening.
- For a natural bleach, make a paste of lemon juice and salt rubbed into a stubborn stain. If it's a nice day let it sit in the sun for a couple of hours.
- Use 1/2 cup of vinegar in a gallon of water as a laundry pre-soak.

In the bathroom:

- Use baking soda instead of toothpaste for excellent oral hygiene.

- A small amount of baking soda on your fingertips makes a fresh feeling, lightly exfoliating daily face wash.
- Vinegar and water in a glass spray bottle work well for surface cleaning.
- Lemon or lime essential oil makes a pleasant smelling disinfectant for the faucet and toilet handles.
- Baking soda is a great toilet cleaner.
- Baking soda and a few drops of the essential oils of your choice added to the bath water make a wonderful, relaxing soak.

For all kinds of non-toxic beauty and self-care products, see Bea Johnson's *Zero Waste Home*.[67]

Mary E. Kingsley

Sample Price and Ingredient Comparison List

(All prices from Amazon.com as of October 2018)

All-Purpose Cleaner:

(kitchen and bath surfaces, floors, appliances, electronics)

Item	Ingredients	Cost
Vinegar/Water (1/2 to 1/2 ratio) in 32 oz. glass spray bottle	Vinegar/Water	$1.60
32 oz. Windex in plastic spray bottle	Water, Isopropyl Alcohol, 2-Hexoxyethanol, Videt EGM, Sodium C14-17 Sec-Alkyl Sulfonate, Ammonium Hydroxide, Propylene Glycol, Mirapol (R) Surf S-210, Fragrance from SC Johnson Fragrance Palette, Liquitint (R)Sky Blue Dye	$5.52

The Lady Farmer Guide to Slow Living

Facial Wash

Item	Ingredients	Cost
Baking Soda in 16 oz cardboard box	Baking Soda	$0.19 per oz
Burt's Bees Radiance Facial Cleanser in 6 oz plastic pump bottle	Aqua (water, eau), decyl glucoside, carthamus tinctorius (safflower) oleosomes, sodium cocoyl hydrolyzed soy protein, glycerin, royal jelly, tocopherol, simmondsia chinensis (jojoba) butter, hydrogenated jojoba oil, vaccinium myrtillus fruit extract, saccharum officinarum (sugar cane, extrait de canne a sucre) extract, acer saccharum (sugar maple) extract, citrus aurantium dulcis (orange) fruit extract, citrus medica limonum (lemon) fruit extract, rosmarinus officinalis (rosemary) leaf extract, gluconic acid, parfum (fragrance), coco-glucoside, glyceryl oleate, glucose, xanthan gum, citric acid, sodium benzoate, sodium chloride, glycine soja (soybean) oil, canola oil (huile de colza), glucose oxidase, lactoperoxidase, butylphenyl methylpropional, hexyl cinnamal, hydroxycitronellal, linalool.	$1.66 per oz

Mary E. Kingsley

TOOTHPASTE

Item	Ingredients	Cost
Baking Soda in 16 oz cardboard box	Baking Soda	$0.19 per oz
Colgate Total Plus Whitening Paste Toothpaste in 7.8 oz plastic tube	Active Ingredients: Sodium Fluoride (0.24% (0.14% w/v Fluoride Ion)), Triclosan (0.30%). Purpose: Anticavity, Antigingivitis. Inactive Ingredients: Water, Hydrated Silica, Glycerin, Sorbitol, PVM/MA Copolymer, Sodium Lauryl Sulfate, Cellulose Gum, Flavor, Sodium Hydroxide, Carrageenan, Propylene Glycol, Sodium Saccharin, Titanium Dioxide.	$0.50 per oz

Clothing Clutter

Clothing is certainly one of the greatest excesses in our personal living spaces, taking up closets, drawers, and multiple storage areas. If you ever lived in a house built before the fast fashion boom, you've probably wondered how in the world the previous inhabitants made do with those tiny closets! That was when people owned much less clothing—they shopped sparingly, chose carefully and made items last. When apparel manufacturing moved overseas and went into mass production mode, the price and quality of clothing plummeted and consumers bought into it to the extent that clothing has become practically disposable. We do well if we have places to put it all and to keep it from spilling over into other spaces. This is not just a problem in our homes, it's a problem for the whole planet considering the enormous amount of clothing discarded by Americans every year. What doesn't end up in the landfill is often "donated" and shipped to other countries where it overwhelms local systems and disrupts local economies by removing demand for domestic products. As well-intentioned as we might be in wanting to pass along our rejects "to someone who can use it," the truth is that in many cases we are sending our waste to be a problem somewhere else.

Where does that leave us in terms of trying to declutter our own lives and spaces? First of all, once we decide to address the problem personally, we can only begin where we are. If you have too many clothes (most of us do!), here are some suggestions for addressing that and for passing your clothes along in perhaps a less wasteful way.

1. Refrain from buying anything new for a season and see how it feels. Do you find yourself lacking in things to wear, or do you find yourself using things you already have in ways you might not have before?

2. If something has been hanging in your closet unworn through a full cycle of seasons, it's most likely that you won't wear it again. If you find yourself thinking "Well, maybe when I lose weight ... or go on a cruise ... or get an invitation to the inaugural ball ..." and so on, ask yourself if it's worth the aggravation of having it in the way and taking up your limited space until those things occur. If you're still uncertain, get a box and put all items in question in it, write the date on it, tape it up and put it out of sight. If in one year you haven't missed any of those things, get rid of it *without opening the box.*

3. To move things out of your house, donate them as locally as possible. For instance, local church rummage sales and thrift stores are more likely to be visited by people in your area who can actually benefit from the clothing you no longer need and keep them out of developing countries or the landfill.

4. Shop at second hand and consignment stores to keep existing clothes in use longer. You will be saving money and keeping your dollars out of the fast fashion sector.

5. When you do decide to buy a new item of clothing, consider a sustainable brand that can account for responsible sourcing and manufacturing. You will likely be spending more per item, but you will be using your buying power to help establish a new consumer paradigm!

Food Clutter

How does it feel when you open your pantry? Is it jammed with various boxes, bottles, half-empty wrappers, packages and cartons? What about the refrigerator? Are there multiple containers of things with multiple ingredients taking up space? Are there mysterious science experiments that live in the back for months at a time? Are you actually using (eating?) most of those things?

Clearing food clutter is greatly simplified if you go at it with the idea of *real* food in mind. Michael Pollan (celebrated food writer and author of *The Omnivore's Dilemma*[68]) says that there's a difference between "real food" and "edible food like substances." Here are some of his suggestions for deciding what to keep and what to pitch.

- Don't eat anything your great-grandmother wouldn't recognize as food. "When you pick up that box of portable yogurt tubes, or eat something with 15 ingredients you can't pronounce, ask yourself, 'What are those things doing there?'"
- Don't eat anything with more than five ingredients, or ingredients you can't pronounce.
- Don't eat anything that won't eventually rot. "There are exceptions — honey — but as a rule, things like Twinkies that never go bad aren't food."

You probably won't get rid of all packaged and processed foods, at least not for a while. These shifts take time. But as you gradually start choosing to fill your kitchen with real food, you'll have fewer boxes and plastic containers to contend with.

Depending on what's available in your area, you might be able to buy things like coffee, nuts, tea, sugar, grains, etc. in bulk and store them in jars. Your refrigerator will be filled with fresh things that get eaten, so you can see what you have and what you need. The fresher the food you buy and eat, the less industry was involved, the less packaging and trash there is and the closer you are to the source of your sustenance. That's slow living.

Section Three Reflections

1. Take some time to walk through the different areas of your home and pay attention to how you feel in each one. Are there spaces where you feel calm and relaxed as opposed to others where you might feel more irritated or anxious? Does your breathing change when you see the pile of papers on the table or too many clothes spilling out of a drawer? Do you close the broom closet as quickly as possible before everything falls out? Pay attention to your thoughts and physical reactions in each space.

2. Use the activity above to identify one trouble area (a table top, drawer, shelf, corner, etc.).

   - Remove all the items leaving empty space and spread them out in another place. Have three bags right beside you as you begin to go through them—one for trash, another for donation and the other for recycling.

   - Take five or ten minutes (time yourself) to look at each item quickly and decide if it can go in one of the bags. If you can't decide immediately that it can be thrown away, donated or recycled, then set it aside.

   - Repeat this process with the reduced pile until you are left with only the things that you absolutely can't let go of at this time.

- Place them back neatly in the designated space, dusting and arranging as you go.
- Notice how that space feels to you now. Hopefully it's more pleasing and peaceful, like you don't mind lingering there.
- Repeat the above process in another problem spot, and then another until eventually you've gone through your whole house.

3. Box it! Take a walk around your house with a medium-sized box. Look around you with a discerning eye and try to spot things that you are fairly neutral about, meaning that you might be able to live without them. These might be clothing items, flower vases, books, candlesticks, pottery, etc. When you find something, put it in the box. Keep doing this until you have collected several items. When it's full, tape the box up, write the date on the top, put it out of sight and forget about it. Don't worry, those things haven't gone anywhere. You can go get them any time you want. The test is this—will you ever even think of them again? If you miss something, by all means reclaim it. But after six months of living without going back to the box, decide to let it go (without opening it) and celebrate the empty space and freedom that you have gained in return.

Conclusion

The Earth As Our Home

A healthy, balanced life necessarily includes some degree of cleanliness, order and respect for where we live. Most of us don't dump nasty things in our living room, poison our own wells, burn things that create bad air in the house, drop trash wherever or destroy things that happen to be in our way.

Yet that's exactly the way humans have behaved on the planet. We're like the terrible tenants that everyone dreads, or those unruly teenagers whose parents are away, the ones who eat up all the food, break the furniture, leave the lights on and the gas tank empty. They don't care what they leave behind because they don't own it.

Why is it that human beings apart from all other creatures on the planet have not demonstrated the care and respect necessary to protect this home we all share, our one and only earth home?

Somewhere along the line, humans began to think, act and live as if we are separate from nature, turning our awareness away from the fact that our existence is dependent on the health and balance of all the interdependent systems sustaining all life on earth. As the dominant species, we have behaved as if it all exists for our own use and benefit, that resources were there to be used up for our immediate gratification and that it doesn't matter what mess we leave behind. And it's catching up with us.

I like to take a hopeful view of this. Maybe it's just a matter of our evolution, and maybe we are at a point as a species where we are growing out of the unruly teenager phase and into an era of respect and ownership. Perhaps humanity is moving closer to a tipping point when our unconscious behavior is no longer the norm. We've all seen pictures of the plastic waste island the size of Texas. We've heard the news that Cape Town is out of water. We've all had friends or family taken way too soon from some cancer that was once rare, but has increased exponentially.

Maybe more of us are teaching our children that food doesn't come from a box and that single use plastic is not okay. Maybe we're all learning to get our hands in the dirt more and sometimes walk barefoot, look at the sky instead of our phones, consider what we put in and on our bodies actually does make a difference.

Perhaps we're moving towards a time when all of humanity respects the one fact that brings us all together. Despite where or how we live on it, the earth is our home—and no matter if we recognize it or not, we will live or die according to how we treat her.

LIST OF RESOURCES

This list is a beginning, a work in progress. Please share with us your additions or suggestions and help us build a comprehensive reference for slow living information, ideas, stories and inspiration.

Books

Food, Herbs and Gardening

Bemis, Andrea. *Dishing Up the Dirt.* Harper Wave, 2017.

Bennett, Robin Rose. *The Gift of Healing Herbs: Plant Medicines and Home Remedies for a Vibrantly Healthy Life.* North Atlantic Books, 2014.

Douillard, John. *The 3-Season Diet: Eat the Way Nature Intended: Lose Weight, Beat Food Cravings, Get Fit.* Harmony, 2007.

Fallon, Sally. *Nourishing Traditions: The Cookbook That Challenges Politically Correct Nutrition and the Diet Dictocrats.* New Trends Publishing, 1999.

Katz, Sandor Ellix. *Wild Fermentation: The Flavor, Nutrition, and Craft of Live-Culture Foods.* Chelsea Green Publishing, 2016.

Morell, Sally Fallon. *Nourishing Broth: An Old-Fashioned Remedy for the Modern World.* Grand Central Life & Style, 2014.

Pollan, Michael. *In Defense of Food: An Eater's Manifesto.* Penguin Books, 2008.

Pollan, Michael. *Omnivore's Dilemma: A Natural History of Four Meals.* Penguin Books, 2006.

Robinson, Jo. *Eating on the Wild Side*. Little, Brown and Company, 2013.

Shanahan, Catherine. *Deep Nutrition: Why Your Genes Need Traditional Food*. Flatiron Books, 2017.

Tickell, Josh. *Kiss the Ground: How the Food You Eat Can Reverse Climate Change*. Atria/Enliven Books, 2017.

Toensmeier, Eric. *Perennial Vegetables: From Artichokes to Zuiki Taro, a Gardner's Guide to Over 100 Delicious and Easy to Grow Edibles*. Chelsea Green Publishing, 2011.

Zachos, Ellen. *Backyard Foraging*. Storey Publishing, LLC, 2013.

CLOTHING

Black, Sandy. *The Sustainable Fashion Handbook*. Thames & Hudson, 2013.

Cline, Elizabeth L. *Overdressed: The Shockingly High Cost of Cheap Fashion*. Portfolio, 2012.

Fletcher, Kate. *Sustainable Fashion and Textiles: Design Journeys*. Routledge, 2014.

Minney, Safia. *Naked Fashion: The New Sustainable Fashion Revolution*. New Internationalist, 2012.

Minney, Safia. *Slow Fashion: Aesthetics Meets Ethics*. New Internationalist, 2016.

Siegle, Lucy. *To Die For: Is Fashion Wearing Out The World?* Fourth Estate, 2011.

SPACES

Berry, Wendell. *The Unsettling of America: Culture & Agriculture*. Counterpoint, 2015.

Johnson, Bea. *Zero Waste Home: The Ultimate Guide to Simplifying Your Life by Reducing Your Waste.* Scribner, 2013.

Kondō, Marie. *The Life-Changing Magic of Tidying up: the Japanese Art of Decluttering and Organizing.* CreateSpace Independent Publishing Platform, 2016.

Linn, Denise. *Sacred Space: Clearing and Enhancing the Energy of Your Home.* Wellspring/Ballantine, 2007.

Madigan, Carleen (ed.). *The Backyard Homestead: Produce All the Food You Need on Just a Quarter Acre!* Storey Publishing, 2009.

Strauss, Erica. *The Hands-On Home: A Seasonal Guide to Cooking, Preserving & Natural Homekeeping.* Sasquatch Books, 2015.

Other

Berry, Thomas. *The Great Work: Our Way into the Future.* Crown, 2011.

Berry, Wendel. *Bringing It To the Table: On Farming and Food.* Counterpoint, 2009.

Childre, Doc, and Howard Martin. *The Heartmath Solution: The Institute of HearthMath's Revolutionary Program for Engaging the Power of the Heart's Intelligence.* HarperOne, 2011.

Hay, Louise L. *You Can Heal Your Life.* Hay House, 1984.

Markegard, Doniga. *Dawn Again: Tracking the Wisdom of the Wild.* Propriometrics Press, 2017.

Miller, Daphne. *Farmacology: Total Health from the Ground Up.* William Morrow Paperbacks, 2016.

Mary E. Kingsley

Documentaries

Kenner, Robert, et al. "Food, Inc.," 2009.
McIlvride, David, et al. "River Blue," 2017.
Morgan, Andrew, et al. "The True Cost," 2015.

Websites and Blogs

www.civileats.com
www.culturedfoodlife.com
www.fashionrevolution.org
www.prairiehomestead.com
www.savory.global
www.slowfood.com
www.slowfoodusa.org
www.theworldinstituteofslowness.com
www.westonaprice.org

Organizations

Civil Eats
EWG (The Environmental Working Group)
Fashion Revolution
Slow Food International
Slow Food USA
The Savory Institute
The Weston Price Foundation
The World Institute of Slowness

21 Day Slow-Living Shift

This is a three-week exercise to help you create fundamental change in the way you feel in your life. It involves about 10 minutes of attention daily. Try not to overthink, take it lightly and have fun!

Getting Started

This exercise starts out with these three powerful paradigm-shifting tools to do every day.

1. Identify your own slow living practice. Maybe it's a few yoga poses, meditation, a cup of coffee by yourself, a Bible verse or two, a few minutes of journaling or a few extra minutes in bed after you wake up. It doesn't matter what it is! What matters is that you get to touch base with YOU every day.

2. Create "gratitude awareness." No need to write anything down (unless you want to!), but cultivate a sense of gratitude about everything around you that you might normally take for granted. For example—running water, sunshine, a car to get you where you need to go, your dog, your bed, your refrigerator, your shoes, your coffee maker, the tree outside your window—the list can go on and on. It's fun to realize how grateful we are for all of these things and to acknowledge it.

3. Develop a "feeling inventory." Start to notice how you are feeling throughout the day. Happy? Irritated? Rushed? Excited? Inspired? Exhausted? Angry? Depressed? Anxious? Whatever your feelings—notice them. Try to stay with the ones that feel good and to shift the not-so-great feelings to better ones. You will get better at this as you work through the following exercises.

Day 1

Take 10 minutes to write down everything that is working in your life. Use this time to generate feelings of goodness and well-being about what *is*, right now. When your mind wants to go to the realities or circumstances that take you away from this, practice moving your thoughts to anything that brings you peace and equilibrium. It is from this place that you will be able to create the desired shifts in your life.

Day 2

Think of one thing in your life, a situation or circumstance, relationship, health concern, whatever it is that pulls you out of well-being. Now list five ways that this is an opportunity for you. Notice how your mind will fight this. Observe the resistance and do it anyway.

Day 3

Describe your current relationship to nature. Where is it satisfying and where is it lacking? What would you like to change about it? Describe a deeply satisfying scene of yourself enjoying nature, something you've actually experienced or something you imagine.

Day 4

Today reflect on your relationship with food. What do you eat? Too much? Too little? What do you love? Do you let yourself have it? Do you spend much of your time thinking about food, or barely any time at all? Do you love to cook or would rather not? There are no right or wrong answers. See what comes to you.

Day 5

Think about your current relationship to clothing. How do you feel about clothes? Where do you get yours? Do they mean a lot to you? Do you shop a lot? Do you have too many? Not enough? Is there conflict with you and your clothes and your body? Again, no right or wrong answers here, just your thoughts.

Day 6

What is your current relationship to your living space? Do you like where you live? Who do you share it with, if anyone? What's right about it? What would you like to change? Describe a favorite spot that makes you feel peaceful. Describe another that creates restlessness or agitation. How would you describe the "energy" of your home?

Day 7

Reflect on exercises #4, 5 and 6. Is there one in particular that created more feeling or emotion than the other? Does there seem to be any conflict regarding your relationship to food, clothing or living spaces? Is there one that is more charged than the other?

Day 8

Repeat the exercise for Day #1. Has it changed at all over the last week?

Day 9

Repeat the exercise for Day #2. Compare your reflections on this from one week ago.

Day 10

Create a scene, as if you were writing a play or a movie script, of something you'd like very much to see happening in your life. Let yourself have fun and enter into it without skepticism or judgment. Just imagine something you'd love to experience and let yourself enjoy all the feelings of it.

Day 11

Reflect on something that makes you feel immensely joyful. Close your eyes and see how long you can sustain that wonderful feeling and imagine it flooding and rejuvenating every cell of your body. Notice the subtle physical sensations that accompany the emotion.

Day 12

Reflect on your personal slow living practice. If it's new to you, write about how it's been for you over the last several days. If it's something you already had in place, write about what it means to you, what it's like for you, anything about it that's a challenge, any observations about it at all.

Day 13

Reflect on how the "gratitude awareness" is going. Write about any thoughts or insights throughout these days.

Day 14

Write about your "feeling inventory." Have you been able to shift from not-so-good to a better feeling place with greater ease than before? Are there any insights or discoveries?

Day 15

Repeat exercise #1.

Day 16

Pick a spot in your house that's disorganized or cluttered and spend 10 minutes clearing it up. Write or reflect on the feelings that it brings.

Day 17

Pick a favorite item of clothing and either wearing it or holding it, spend 10 minutes thinking or writing about where it came from, who made it, how long you've worn it, experiences you've had wearing it. Imagine what it would be like to have that same awareness and care for all of your clothing.

Day 18

Select one food today and spend a full 10 minutes eating it with your full attention. As you take a bite, let it linger in your mouth as you feel its texture, experience its taste and slowly let it enter your body. Ask yourself, where did it come from? What's in it? Who prepared it? How far has it traveled? What is the story behind it? How is it going to nourish me? Write about your experience if you wish.

Day 19

Spend 10 minutes today giving your full attention to something in nature or to an animal. Stare at a tree or a flower or pet your dog or cat. Reflect on what this is like for you. Was it relaxing? Did you feel impatient, or that you should be doing something else? Did it affect the rest of your day in any way?

Day 20

Repeat Day #10.

Day 21

Reflect on the last three weeks of these exercises. What's been valuable for you? What's come up? Has anything changed? It's said that 21 days is enough time to change a habit. If you've stuck to your slow living practice, your gratitude awareness and your feelings inventory, maybe you're beginning to see a shift towards greater peace and contentment in your every day. If you like it, start again and keep going. We'd love to hear your insights and suggestions as you explore what slow living means for you and your life.

About the Author

Mary was born in Kingsport, Tennessee surrounded by the hills of southern Appalachia. Writing, a sense of place, and the desire to share experience have always been important to her journey, and play critical roles as she continues to weave her personal narrative. With the kids grown and three works of fiction as of this writing (*Angel, All the Pieces* and *Dear Jeannette*), she and her husband decided to realize a long-held dream and made the move to a small farm in Maryland. The homesteading lifestyle has fit her like a pen to paper, as she spends the better part of every day outside, living and learning close to the rhythms of the natural world. It has taught her that life is better, healthier and happier when we bring heart and passion to the basics. Being intentional about how we feed and clothe ourselves and ultimately how we live is her day-to-day goal. That's why she teamed up with daughter Emma in 2016 to create Lady Farmer, a sustainable apparel and lifestyle brand, which has been growing a community of conscious creators in an exciting new paradigm of intentional, sustainable living.

Works Cited

1. Berry, Thomas Mary. *The Great Work: Our Way into the Future.* Bell Tower, 2000.
2. Pollan, Michael. *Food Rules: An Eater's Manual.* Penguin Books, 2009.
3. Lloyd, Robin. "First Humans: Time of Origin Pinned Down." *LiveScience*, Purch, 23 Feb. 2007, https://www.livescience.com/4406-humans-time-origin-pinned.html.
4. Lloyd, Robin. "First Humans: Time of Origin Pinned Down." *LiveScience*, Purch, 23 Feb. 2007, https://www.livescience.com/4406-humans-time-origin-pinned.html.
5. "The Development of Agriculture." *Genographic Project*, "Donna's Live Sourdough Culture." *Cultured Food Life*, https://genographic.nationalgeographic.com/development-of-agriculture/.
6. "The Homestead Act of 1862." *National Archives and Records Administration*, National Archives and Records Administration https://www.archives.gov/education/lessons/homestead-act.
7. Babcock, Jillian. "Diagram Shows How to Create Your Very Own 'Food Forest' (Better Than Organic!)." *Dr. Axe*, Dr. Axe, 29 Sept. 2017, https://draxe.com/permaculture/.
8. Fallon, Sally, et al. *Nourishing Traditions: the Cookbook That Challenges Politically Correct Nutrition and the Diet Dictocrats.* NewTrends Publishing, Inc., 2005.

9   Strauss, Erica. *Hands-on Home*. Sasquatch Books, 2015.

10 Dupont, Veronique. "Nitrates Poison Water in California's Central Valley." Phys.Org, 20 Sept. 2016, https://phys.org/news/2016-09-nitrates-poison-california-central-valley.html.

11 Pirello, Christina. "Is the Early Onset of Puberty in Young Girls Linked to Meat?" *The Huffington Post*, TheHuffingtonPost.com, 17 Nov. 2011, https://www.huffpost.com/entry/is-the-early-onset-of-pub_b_677424.

12 Price, Annie. "6 Grass-Fed Beef Nutrition Benefits that May Surprise You." *Dr. Axe*, Dr. Axe, 31 Jan. 2018, https://draxe.com/grass-fed-beef-nutrition/.

13 Environmental Working Group. "Why Go Organic, Grass-Fed and Pasture-Raised?" *EWG*, https://www.ewg.org/meateatersguide/a-meat-eaters-guide-to-climate-change-health-what-you-eat-matters/why-go-organic-grass-fed-and-pasture-raised/.

14 Morell, Sally Fallon. *Nourishing Broth: An Old-Fashioned Remedy for the Modern World*. Grand Central Life & Style, 2014.

15 Realmilk.com, Webmaster. "Key Documents." *A Campaign for Real Milk*, 4 Oct. 2016, http://www.real-milk.com/key-documents/.

16 Realmilk.com, Webmaster. "More About Raw Milk." *A Campaign for Real Milk*, 4 Feb. 2014, http://www.real-milk.com/health/more-about-raw-milk/.

17 Whoriskey, Peter. "Why Your 'Organic' Milk May Not Be Organic." *The Washington Post*, WP Company, 1 May 2017, https://www.washingtonpost.com/business/economy/why-your-organic-milk-may-not-be-organic/2017/05/01/708ce5bc-ed76-11e6-9662-6eedf1627882_story.html.

18 Certified Humane. "How to Buy the Healthiest Eggs." *Certified Humane*, 26 July, 2010, https://certifiedhumane.org/how-to-buy-the-healthiest-eggs/.

19 Whoriskey, Peter. "People Love Chickens That Are 'Vegetarian Fed.' But Chickens Are Not Vegetarians." *The Washington Post*, WashingtonPost.com, 29 Apr. 2015, https://www.washingtonpost.com/news/wonk/wp/2015/04/29/consumers-love-chickens-that-are-vegetarian-fed-never-mind-what-the-birds-want-to-eat/.

20 A Greener World. "Certified Animal Welfare Approved by AGW| A Greener World." *Agreenerworld.org*, https://agreenerworld.org/certifications/animal-welfare-approved/.

21 Certified Humane. "Certified Humane Raised and Handled." *CertifiedHumane.org*, https://certifiedhumane.org/.

22 Certified Humane. "'Free Range' and 'Pasture Raised' Officially Defined by HFAC for Certified Humane Label." *Certified Humane*, 16 Jan. 2014, https://certifiedhumane.org/free-range-and-pasture-raised-officially-defined-by-hfac-for-certified-humane-label/.

23 Robinson, Jo. *Eating on the Wild Side: the Missing Link to Optimum Health*. Little, Brown and Company, 2014.

24 Robinson, Jo. *Eating on the Wild Side: the Missing Link to Optimum Health*. Little, Brown and Company, 2014.

25 "10 Dandelion Root Health Benefits." *Real Food For Life*, 29 Oct. 2017, http://www.realfoodforlife.com/dandelion-root-health-benefits/.

26 Stephenson, Karen. "Garlic Mustard Pesto Recipe." *Edible Wild Food Blog*, http://www.ediblewildfood.com/garlic-mustard-pesto-recipe.aspx.

27 Edible Wild Food. "Welcome to Edible Wild Food." *EdibleWildFood.com*, http://www.ediblewildfood.com/

28 Bourrie, Benjamin C.T., et al. "The Microbiota and Health Promoting Characteristics of the Fermented Beverage Kefir." *Frontiers*, Frontiers, 18 Apr. 2016, https://www.frontiersin.org/articles/10.3389/fmicb.2016.00647/full.

29 Schwenk, Donna. "Welcome To Cultured Food Life!" *Cultured Food Life*, https://www.culturedfoodlife.com/.

30 Katz, Sandor Ellix. *Wild Fermentation: the Flavor, Nutrition, and Craft of Live-Culture Foods*. Chelsea Green Pub., 2016.

31 *The Holy Bible: Revised Standard Version*. Thomas Nelson Publishing for Ignatius Press, 2006.

32 NY Fashion Center. "The History of Fabric and Textiles." *NY Fashion Center Fabrics*, https://www.nyfashioncenterfabrics.com/pages/history-of-fabric-and-textiles.

33 "The Rise of American Industry." *Ushistory.org*, Independence Hall Association, http://www.ushistory.org/us/25.asp.

34 Perry, Patsy. "The Environmental Costs of Fast Fashion." *The Independent.* Independent.co.uk, 8 January 2018. https://www.independent.co.uk/life-style/fashion/environment-costs-fast-fashion-pollution-waste-sustainability-a8139386.html

35 "The True Cost." *The True Cost*, https://truecostmovie.com/learn-more/human-rights/.

36 "Home." *Fashion Revolution*, https://www.fashionrevolution.org/.

37 Jordan Harper. Nivelo. www.nivelo.co.uk. *Ethical Fashion Forum*, https://the.ethicalfashionforum.com/.

38 Ross, Michael, et al. *The True Cost.* 2015.

39 Blum, Deborah. "Fashion at a Very High Price." *The New York Times*, The New York Times, 20 Dec. 2013, https://well.blogs.nytimes.com/2013/12/20/fashion-at-a-very-high-price/.

40 Boddy, Jessica. "Are We Eating Our Fleece Jackets? Microfibers Are Migrating Into Field And Food." *NPR*, 6 Feb. 2017, https://www.npr.org/sections/the-salt/2017/02/06/511843443/are-we-eating-our-fleece-jackets-microfibers-are-migrating-into-field-and-food.

41 Krupnick, Ellie. "Chemicals In Fast Fashion Revealed in Greenpeace's 'Toxic Threads: The Big Fashion Stitch-Up.'" *The Huffington Post*, TheHuffingtonPost.com, 29 Nov. 2012, https://www.huffpost.com/entry/chemicals-in-fast-fashion-greenpeace-toxic-thread_n_2166189.

42 Winn, Patrick. "The Slave Labor behind Your Favorite Clothing Brands: Gap, H&M and More Exposed." *Salon*, Salon.com, 20 Mar. 2015, https://www.salon.com/2015/03/22/the_slave_labor_behind_your_favorite_clothing_brands_gap_hm_and_more_exposed_partner/.

43 "The True Cost." *The True Cost*, https://truecostmovie.com/learn-more/environmental-impact/.

44 "North American Free Trade Agreement (NAFTA)." *Panama-U.S. FTA Overview | Public Citizen*, https://www.citizen.org/our-work/globalization-and-trade/north-american-free-trade-agreement-nafta.

45 Kane, Mari. "The Four Basic Uses of Cannabis Hemp: Food, Fiber, Fuel, Medicine." *Hemp Traders,* http://www.hemptraders.com/Hemp-101-s/1883.htm.

46 "General Hemp Information, Uses, Facts." *Hemp Basics*, https://www.hempbasics.com/shop/hemp-information.

47 "History of Hemp." *Hemp.com*, http://www.hemp.com/history-of-hemp/.

48 Steenstra, Eric. "Industrial Hemp: An Ancient Crop with Potential for Today's Farmers." 8 Nov. 2018. University of Maryland Agricultural Law Conference. http://umaglaw.org/download/industrial-hemp-an-ancient-crop-with-potential-for-todays-farmers-steenstra/.

49 "Marihuana Tax Act of 1937." *Wikipedia*, Wikimedia Foundation, 10 June 2018, https://en.wikipedia.org/wiki/Marihuana_Tax_Act_of_1937.

50 Kentucky Hempsters. "Hemp 101: What Is Hemp, What's It Used for, and Why Is It Illegal?" *Leafly*, 25 Aug. 2017, https://www.leafly.com/news/cannabis-101/hemp-101-what-is-hemp-whats-it-used-for-and-why-is-it-illegal.

51 United States Congress, Johnson, Renee. "Hemp as an Agricultural Commodity." *Hemp as an Agricultural Commodity*, 2017. https://fas.org/sgp/crs/misc/RL32725.pdf.

52 "Hemp Farming Legalized Across the United States by the 2018 Farm Bill." *Vote Hemp*. VoteHemp.com, 20 Dec. 2018, https://www.votehemp.com/press_releases/hemp-farming-legalized-across-the-united-states-by-the-2018-farm-bill/.

53 "Feels Right, Naturally." *TENCEL*, https://www.tencel.com/.

54 Cotton Today. *Cotton*, https://cottontoday.cottoninc.com/.

55 Wallander, Mattias. "Organic Cotton: Threading Its Way Into Our Closets." *The Huffington Post*, TheHuffingtonPost.com, 16 Apr. 2014, https://www.huffingtonpost.com/mattias-wallander/organic-cotton-threading-_b_4784430.html.

56 Cotton Today. *Cotton*, https://cottontoday.cottoninc.com/.

57 Baldwin, Peyton. "Why Organic Cotton Is Better." 3 Jun. 2008, *Mother Earth News,* https://www.motherearthnews.com/nature-and-environment/environmental-policy/organic-cotton-benefits.

58 Fibershed. "About: Our Mission and Vision." www.fibershed.com/about/.

59 Messinger, Leah. "How Your Clothes Are Poisoning Our Oceans and Food Supply." *The Guardian*. TheGuardian.com, 20 Jun. 2016, https://www.theguardian.com/environment/2016/jun/20/microfibers-plastic-pollution-oceans-patagonia-synthetic-clothes-microbeads.

60 Moore, Lorrie. *Like Life*. Faber and Faber, 2010.

61 Berry, Wendell. *Farming: a Handbook*. Harcourt, Brace, Jovanovich, 1970.

62 Aslett, Don. *Clutter's Last Stand: It's Time to De-Junk Your Life!* Adams Media, 2005.

63 Morgenstern, Julie. *Organizing from the Inside Out*. Henry Holt and Co., 1998.

64 Kondō, Marie. *The Life-Changing Magic of Tidying up: the Japanese Art of Decluttering and Organizing*. CreateSpace Independent Publishing Platform, 2016.

65 Harris, Alexander, et al. "Self-Storage Industry Statistics." *The SpareFoot Blog*, 27 Mar. 2018, https://www.sparefoot.com/self-storage/news/1432-self-storage-industry-statistics/.

66 Home Organization Market in the US - Demand and Sales Forecasts, Market Share, Market Size, Market Leaders." *The Freedonia Group*, https://www.freedoniagroup.com/Home-Organization-Products.html.

67 Johnson, Bea. *Zero Waste Home: the Ultimate Guide to Simplifying Your Life*. Particular Books, 2016.

68 Pollan, Michael. *The Omnivore's Dilemma a Natural History of Four Meals*. Penguin Books, 2016.

www.ingramcontent.com/pod-product-compliance
Lightning Source LLC
Chambersburg PA
CBHW021953290426
44108CB00012B/1049